An Empty Spoon

An Empty Spoon

by SUNNY DECKER

photographs by TANA HOBAN

1817

Harper & Row, Publishers
New York, Evanston, and London

LIBRARY OF CONGRESS CATALOG CARD NUMBER: 69–15305

To Rob and the kids

AUTHOR'S NOTE

I guess it's important to note that all the names in this book—with the exception of public figures—are entirely fictitious, and any resemblance to the names of living persons is wholly coincidental.

I know it's important to note that there are people who helped to make this book—Robert Decker, Marjorie Morris, Samuel Schwartz, Evan Thomas, Jane Wickett, Gene Young. To them, my thanks for their effort, inspiration, and an occasional kick in the pants.

S. D.

The photographs in this book were taken by Tana Hoban. They have been placed in the text at random, and the people portrayed in the photographs are not those described in the adjacent text.

I went about to fil your
mouth with an empty spoone:
That is, to seeme to teach,
not to teach.

Stefano Guazzo, 1574

The First Year

Life is not a bowl of cherries
It's a bowl of love, and
hate and misunderstanding

M Y SIXTH-PERIOD class was weird. Five months of living with them had provided lots of time to get to know the kids, since there were only thirty-five on roll, with about twenty showing up. But they were a strange bunch, and they lacked that feeling of group-ness that classes usually develop. These eleventh-graders had somehow remained isolated from one another. There was no class personality.

Haughty Mae Hall was a toughy. She was tall and lean, and was the only girl in school who wore slacks. Sometime during the year, she'd had her front teeth knocked out, and she didn't even care. She was mean once in a while, but not often, and she did beautiful work. So we got along O.K.

Algy Brown was the closest thing I ever had to a discipline problem. It figures, with a name like Algy. He never shut his mouth, and took great pride in his ability to disrupt a class in twenty seconds flat. He had a great sense of humor, and I always enjoyed him—except

1

when he hurt my feelings with a nasty crack. He never did any work. He just sat next to Bernice and made noise. And Bernice went along with him, except when we did dictionary work or some other dull, rote thing. She liked that kind of stuff. Bernice was mysterious. Her words and expressions were guarded, and she kept everyone at a distance. She was unusually bright. But she kept failing, because the only stuff she'd turn in was dictionary work.

The fat, ugly kid in the back of the room was Diana Ricks. All she did was suck her thumb. And all Robert Jones ever did was intimidate me, with his quiet, searching eyes.

Elvira Jackman was really beautiful, when she did something with her hair. She wore the same clothes every day, all year. She used to hang around my desk before class and tell me secrets—like Mary Ward likes girls. But since I liked Mary Ward, I didn't care. She was the only A student in the class. And the only thing about her that bothered me was her stray eye. It sure was ugly.

One day before class, I heard a commotion in the hall outside my room, and went out to see what was going on. Mary and Elvira had squared off and were obviously ready to tear each other apart. When boys fight, there's little commotion. They just cut each other and go away. But the girls are vicious. I was glad I knew both these girls. All I had to do was get them into class, and we'd talk about it. I walked over to them and suggested they come into the room. They never took their eyes off each other. But they both began to talk at once—accusing each other and telling me to move away. I wasn't scared—after all, they were my girls. But I was awed at the strength and hatred they generated. A crowd began to gather. Once they had an audience, they had to perform. The girls came to watch because they love a good fight. The boys came in the hope that clothes would be ripped off and they'd get a good look at some bare body. The hall was packed.

I spotted someone I knew in the crowd and told her to get some teachers to clear the corridor. I couldn't understand why they hadn't come already—the noise was more than enough to attract attention. After an endless wait, the girl returned, saying none of the teachers on the hall would help—they'd closed their doors. My God, how can a bunch of adults be afraid of kids? And how can they find it in themselves to ignore what's obviously an emergency situation?

"Come on, Mrs. Decker," Mary was saying. "I don't want to hurt you. You better get away."

"Please come with me," I begged. "You're only going to get yourself in trouble."

"I'm gonna kill that bitch," Elvira was wailing. Her eyes were full of tears and fury. I thought I saw the point of a can opener in her hand.

The crowd was pressing in on us. I couldn't just stand there forever, holding things in limbo. The mob in the hall was as dangerous as the girls they encircled. So I backed out and ran to the phone in my room. That was when the fight started. Before too long, there were police and male teachers breaking up the mob. I couldn't see what was happening inside the circle. I could only try to get kids on the periphery to go to class. That in itself was a difficult task. I felt I had to be superpolite. It would have been stupid to play authoritarian—I didn't have one shred of authority, and we all knew it.

By the time I got to the girls, they were different people. Their hair stuck out from their heads in ugly clumps. Mary's blouse was torn to shreds. Elvira was bleeding from somewhere on her face. And she was hysterical. Each girl was being held against a wall by two men. Their eyes were wild. The hall was quiet now, and I spoke to each of them, trying to calm them. They quieted a little. The fight was over.

It was then that Morris started. Morris Feldman is fat and dumb. He teaches science, I think, and people talk about his tendency to "mishandle" situations. He was one of the men holding Elvira. It seemed that he felt personally threatened in some way by what had happened. Or maybe he just hates kids. Or blacks. He glared at her with his bulgy eyes, and his puffy mouth called her an animal. He terrified me. The biggest trouble with people is that they're people. Few of us ever deal with trying situations without expressing our own feelings. It's hard to be a professional. But Morris never even tried. Before I knew it, he'd grabbed Elvira by the hair and dragged her down a flight of steps. She was mad with fury, screaming and flailing her arms and legs. He just pulled her down, hair first. I chased them.

"For God's sake," I was screaming, "will you let her stand still for a minute—will you treat her like a human being!"

"Well Goddamn it—" he was all purpley—"if you're so damn smart, you take her!" He grabbed the girl by the shoulders and threw her at me. I nearly fell. When he'd stormed off, Elvira and I sat down on the step and shook. The girl's hysteria had vanished when she saw me threatened. She just kept crying and saying, "It's all right—don't worry—it's all right."

A teaching aide took Elvira to wash her face before she went to the discipline office. My department head found me on the steps and told me to make a report of the fight to the vice principal. Someone would cover my class.

I wanted to cry, but I was too embarrassed. I'd all but forgotten the fight by then. I just kept seeing that hideous, fat bully brutalizing my kid. As I approached the vice principal's office another science teacher stopped me. He acted quiet and a little strange.

"I don't know what you're going to say in there," he began. "But if you're smart, you won't mention what happened after the fight. Unless you want to press charges, of course. And things could get unpleasant if you did that." He walked away. I didn't know what the hell was going on. I was shaking like mad.

I never got to the vice principal's office. The Disciplinarian called me into her office to report on the girls. Mary and Elvira were sitting on opposite sides of the room. The woman said there was some question about weapons, and had I seen a can opener in Elvira's possession. She explained that both girls would be suspended for fighting, but that if there were weapons, they would be sent to jail.

I said I couldn't be sure I'd seen anything. She didn't believe me, but that was all right. Again, I wanted to cry. It was nerves. I can cope during a crisis, but I fall apart afterward. The girls said they were sorry I had to be involved, and that they wouldn't make any more trouble. I said I didn't expect them to, and went back to class.

Algy Brown was absent, so there was no comic relief at all. The kids are very sensitive to my moods, and I just couldn't talk. I sat at my desk, while the kids squirmed. I'd never behaved that way, and they didn't know what to do with me.

Haughty played with the cuff on her pants, and the others watched one another and me. Diana just sucked her thumb. Bernice read a dictionary. The bell finally rang.

From then on, I felt the class was more of a unit. Lovida Barr began to talk to Diana, and perhaps Diana sucked her thumb a little less. Haughty was pleasant to Elvira and Mary, because they'd proved they could really fight. But Robert Jones was as stern and pensive as ever, and Raymond Tibbs still sat next to the window alone. I had never been able to get him to speak. He'd never smiled. His work, what little he did, was awful. He spelled his name differently every time he wrote it. He seemed like the loneliest guy in the whole world.

Later in the term, he began to sleep in class. I thought it was a rude way of telling me what a bore I was. Then I found out that he slept in subways at night, because he couldn't face going home. There were thirteen hungry kids there. His father was an alcoholic. He hadn't seen his mother in two years. He spent his afternoons stealing food at supermarkets, but they were getting wise to him. If he went home empty-handed, his father would beat him. So he slept in subways.

February third. Enter Frankie Horn. When I asked where he'd been for the first half of the year, he said he had been kicked out of Marshall High when he went on trial for rape. I asked him if he'd raped the girl. He said no. Frankie was tall and handsome, though he had a mustache I didn't particularly care for. I didn't expect much from him. He seemed honest and interesting, but I never would have pegged him for a student. I was wrong. He did every assignment and became an important force in the class. He could generate discussion among the other kids—something I'd been unable to do. With the exception of Diana and Raymond, they all talked to me, but I never could step out of a discussion and let the kids carry it. Not until Frankie came.

Only Bernice seemed uncomfortable about the growing spirit in class. I don't know whether she reacted to Frankie personally, or whether she felt that discussions put her in a vulnerable position. But she grew increasingly unpleasant and refused to read assigned books, write compositions, or smile. She'd answer factual questions; never did she allow any of Bernice to expose herself. Since Algy had disappeared in late winter, she sat alone. I would have given anything to know what was going on inside her.

In early spring two new girls were transferred into the class. They sauntered into the room and sat together near the rear wall. When I asked them their names, they told me I ought to know since I was the teacher. It was going to be a difficult hour.

I handed out paper, and the girls let it slide to the floor. I asked the class to take out pens; the girls began to crack their gum. They made snide remarks about everything. The other kids never said a word the whole period. They just sat and stared at me, and I had wild visions of the whole group uniting against me—a teacher always makes a good scapegoat.

"I'll bet she thinks she's pretty cute," one of the girls muttered just loudly enough.

"I wonder who thought up that stupid assignment," the other said. I had to ignore them. To compete would have been fatal—I'm just not clever enough. So I said nothing—but they were plenty hard to ignore.

By the time the bell rang, I hated every kid I'd ever met, and decided it might be nice to work in a toy store or something. I was about to dash to the bathroom when Frankie and Bernice approached me. I didn't know what to expect.

"Mrs. Decker," Frankie began. He looked at me very hard. "We've got to get those girls out of here." I couldn't believe it.

"You're gonna not like them, and you won't want to teach us any more," Bernice said.

"We've got something sort of special in this class," Frankie continued, "and we're not gonna let them ruin it."

Great things happen at the funniest times.

I asked what they thought we should do. Frankie said, "Don't you worry about it—I'll take care of them after school."

I explained that dealing with people is tough business, and you can't just kill everyone you don't like. They finally agreed that more subtle tactics might be better. And besides, it wasn't worth it to get yourself in trouble over such jive people. I said I'd leave it to the class to handle the situation. It was an easy way out. It made them feel good—and I hadn't the slightest idea what to do myself.

By the next day, the underground was organized. The kids came in to class and scattered themselves around the room. When the victims walked in, they couldn't find seats together. Delightful! I'd never even thought of the divide-and-conquer tactic.

It was a tense class. Everyone seemed waiting for a chance to make his move. At the first bitchy remark of the day, Haughty Mae stood up and put one hand on her hip and said in a very slurry, dramatic way, "Pardon me, but the teacher is trying to teach." She sat down like a queen. It was probably the first time in her life she'd fought without fists. She seemed as pleased with herself as I was.

It was a long hour, but by the end, it was obvious that the balance of power had changed. By the end of the week the girls had begun to do some work. A week later, one of them smiled at me. I smiled back, and the day after she was perched on my desk showing me snapshots of her boyfriend. Frankie walked in on the scene, and gave me a very grownup-type smile. He'd won, and he wasn't even gloating.

Of all the things I've tried to do in class, Japanese haiku was the most rewarding. Almost none of the kids could write a decent essay. Few of them could handle a paragraph—they just didn't have the skills. The great thing about haiku was that it was so short and so highly structured; it forced them to make a meaningful statement in a small space. I introduced it to the sixth period with a trumped-up story about the samurai soldiers, who, though they were the smallest soldiers in the world, could never be defeated. Why? Because they used their wits—how else could they have invented judo and karate? Anyway, to sharpen their wits, they would sit around the palace and compose these word puzzles—called haiku. I presented it strictly in game terms. If I'd slipped and said poetry I'd have blown the whole bit.

The kids wrote wonderful things. And when I put their haikus on the board and discussed the hidden meanings, their faces would light up. They couldn't articulate their intentions themselves—but they sure knew what they meant.

From the quiet Robert, I got:

> I think not of death
> For it is a privilege
> I who am a slave

Haughty Mae rolled a toothpick in the space where her teeth had been and wrote,

> You try to hurt me
> Destroy all things about me
> Me! I will just laugh!

and later,

> Can't walk down the street
> Because someone will grab you
> That's no kind of life

Diana still sucked her thumb, but she began to work:

> A baby is born
> Love and care are needed
> How will it live?

And Mary was still fighting:

> Young punks scared to die
> There's nothing to it—just croak!
> I cry night and day.

Even Raymond Tibbs found a voice:

> The world is alive now
> They can see and hear
> Why can't they feel?

> In everyone's life
> There's lots of togetherness
> What happened to mine?

And Bernice finally closed her dictionary.

> Love leaves a black spot
> Which takes time to erase
> Hate is easier

There was a paper with no name. It seemed appropriate.

> Believe and exist
> I always believe
> I died believing

Late in the spring, Algy Brown appeared at my door. He said he'd been in a mental hospital. He'd tried to commit suicide. I told him he didn't look like the type and was he coming back to school. He didn't know. He was sort of messed up, 'cause he'd just found out that the man he'd known as his father was really his uncle, and the man he'd called uncle was his father. He was having trouble keeping his mind on schoolwork. He just wanted to come and visit, because he missed me.

I said I'd missed him too, and if there was anything at all I could do—

He left reluctantly, but with a smile. I never saw him again.

That's the way it was with most of the kids, once the term was over. A lot of them moved, or dropped out. Some passed you in the hall the next year and seemed shocked when you remembered them. As if they never expected you to.

It's funny that I should have memories like this. I'd always hated school, and staying there, even on the other side of the desk, was a gruesome idea. My family had moved to the suburbs so I could have the benefit of "an exceptional public education"—and with the exception of Miss Simpson in sixth grade and Miss Peabody in ninth, I would have gladly burned that whole collection of Main Line matrons and their copies of *Ivanhoe*.

Teachers were such gray people—gray suits, gray skin, gray personalities. They taught from yellowed notes they'd made up thirty years ago, and hated all the Negroes and Jews that were moving to the

Philadelphia Main Line. Things just weren't what they used to be, what with the "new element" and all.

It didn't take long to realize that my school's reputation arose from the caliber of its students—not the quality of its teachers. We were just a damn smart bunch of kids, and our parents had reared us to believe that college was part of our compulsory education. So we produced.

I was the only kid I knew who ever got a D on a report card. It was in French. My teacher was a crazy lady. Her hair was a different color every week. She picked her nose. Anyway, she started screaming one day in front of the whole class that I was *très stupide*, that I shouldn't go to college—that I should work in Woolworth's. So I started cutting class. That's how I got my D.

By twelfth grade everything about school annoyed me—even the kids I'd grown up with. I was bored to death with record hops and choir practice, and thus a bit uncomfortable—it's no fun to feel like a misfit. So I played hooky three days a week—Monday, Wednesday, and Friday—till I got caught. It took them a long time to catch up with me. I mean, in a school like Lower Merion, they just weren't attuned to such problems.

Cutting is a huge problem at North High. The kids cut something like four thousand classes a week, which isn't so awful if you realize they're keeping a staff of four employed. The sad part of our cutting problem is that so few kids do it as a prank. They don't begin to enjoy the thrill of getting away with something as I did. Lavell Keller was like that.

He was the littlest boy I ever saw—little and fragile. His hair and eyes and skin were all the same soft color. I don't think I ever heard him speak. He began to cut my class the second day of school. I guess he came the first day to check out my legs.

The school has an elaborate system for reporting cuts that requires poring over a list of more than a thousand names every day. I liked to think that my class was so exciting that no one would cut—and those who did would not be worthy additions anyway. So, for a month, I never even checked the list.

I woke up, of course. To the fact that, given the chance, I would cut even the best of classes—my record attested to that; to the fact that I was allowing kids who were begging for discipline to hang themselves; to the fact that I was lazy.

I began to check. It was hard as hell. I had to play a match game for every absentee on my roll of two hundred students. If they were really out of school, their names would be somewhere on The List. If they weren't on it, they were cutting. For each cutter, I had to fill out a slip and send it to the petty-crimes office. It was their job to track down the offenders and discipline them appropriately. A messy process.

But before long, I got compulsive about it. I came to school early just to find out who had cut me the day before. I reported the crimes with incredible efficiency. I must have written a pound of cut slips on poor Lavell Keller.

Months passed before I realized that attendance in my classes had increased. I hadn't looked for constructive ends. I took no joy in being an authoritarian, either. It's just that once I knew a kid cut my class, my feelings got hurt—and I wanted to get him back.

It wasn't easy to wage war with Lavell. He didn't mind the detentions (you just sit there) or suspensions (a three-day holiday with the school's blessing) that the cutting office assigned him. If he'd minded, he would have come to class.

I never saw him again until March, when I was asked to patrol the cafeteria. There he was, with a hot dog in his fist.

I was pretty nice, considering the months of humiliation I'd undergone because of him. I gave him the usual spiel, and asked the usual questions. Lavell said nothing. He looked way up at me and made me feel big and gawky, so I ended my harangue with an end-of-harangue-type summation, and walked away.

One of the counselors had seen me with Lavell, and asked if there was a problem. "A problem!" I was shrieky. "He hasn't been in English class since September!"

"But my dear, of course not," she said. "Don't you see—Lavell can't read a word."

I saw. I was not the object of hostility. I was only the mirror that would show Lavell his failures. And who wants to see failure every day at nine in the morning. I didn't bother to ask how in hell he ever got to the tenth grade, or why no one ever told me he had a problem. That's an old bureaucratic story by now.

I tried to find him in the crowded lunchroom, to tell him that I might help him if he'd give me the chance. But he'd disappeared.

Though I still got mad at kids who cut me, I was a little more careful now, about checking reasons as well as cuts, and I was a little less ruthless. And though I'd learned something from Lavell, I felt crummy about making him an object lesson.

I still think about him from time to time. He got an F in English for the year. And then he dropped out of school.

My motivation for cutting was, of course, different from Lavell's. I didn't drop out. I managed to get straight A's my senior year. The principal, a man I'd never seen until I became a Problem, had explained to me that my board scores were way too high in relation to my grades, and no college wanted an underachiever. Since I wanted to go to Swarthmore, I saw to it that I got the A's. Swarthmore wasn't impressed. I went to Penn.

I don't know why my attitude toward school didn't change when I got to college. I had some awfully good courses, achieved like mad, and graduated with honors. But I still cut all the classes I could, and much preferred sitting under a tree or eating cheeseburgers to intellectualizing. I went through college doggedly. Every A I got meant, "See—I'm not cut out for Woolworth's." What a dumb way to spend $10,000. And the irony of it was that my Ivy League degree equipped me to do nothing more than peddle dime-store products—I couldn't even type.

There was another embarrassing complication. I'd spent years wisecracking about girls who go to college to find husbands and teach to put them through graduate school. I'd spent years fighting my family tooth and nail about taking education courses—which were only for dumb, coed-type females. Then I blew the whole bit and got married the day before graduation. It was humiliating. The whole world could call me typical. If only I could have lived without him.

Since Rob had three years of graduate school ahead of him, I knew I was stuck with Philadelphia for a while.

Actually, it's a fine city. My only gripe was that I wanted to live in as many worlds as possible, and I felt ready for a change. I could never understand why so many people are content to live and die in the same place they were born. I was always telling my classes about places like California and pushing them to strike out on their own. I would tell them how easy it would be to hitch across the country and work on a ranch out West, or get a job on a boat and sail the Virgin Islands. They would say things like, "No driver with sense picks up a nigger on a highway." Or, "It's not so easy to take a trip when your mother needs you to help feed ten kids."

When I taught them how to write a business letter, I brought in addresses of camps, resorts, ranches and sea captains, and made everyone apply for a summer job. I thought if just a couple of kids would spend a month in the mountains, the whole project would have been justified. When Sedrick Powell started to get excited about working on a dude ranch in Colorado, I told him we'd take him there, since we were driving West for the summer. He never mailed his letter. I don't think anyone else did either. For kids who've seen so much of life, they sure are scared. I want them to know the world isn't all ghetto and gang war, but they just don't venture into new waters.

King Copeley was one of the hardest guys to get to. He was no more than a name on the rolls for the first month of school. When he finally made his appearance, he sat in the back of the room and stared. He made me squirm. He was very black, and his eyes seemed as scarred from life as his face was from knives. He wore a Jewish star around his thick neck on a leather thong. A gold earring was looped through one ear.

It took me a good half-hour to get up the nerve to approach him. His stare wasn't really hostile, but it was more than I could handle. I was coming unstrung. I walked to his seat and spoke quietly. I didn't want to put him in the position of being challenged in front of the whole class.

"Are you ready to do some work?" I asked.

"Thanks anyway, but I'll wait till tomorrow." That sounded reasonable. I was content to let him pick his own time. It meant he'd take care of himself without my badgering him. It meant he was indeed planning to do some work.

King wasn't really responsible for the hostility that grew between us. He was simply silent. I was the one who couldn't hack it. I tried everything from humor to antagonism to get a reaction. Nothing.

I don't remember the precise turning point, but it was shortly after he walked out of class. Just got up and left. We had it out later that day in the hall. I told him he was rude. He said I'd insulted him with a crack I'd made about people with big ears.

"Why? Are your ears big?" I felt ridiculous. Here we were, making an issue over this dumb thing. Big ears! But we'd begun to talk.

King Solomon Copeley opened up a lot during the next months. He told me he was an Ethiopian Jew, and spoke fluent Hebrew. He'd just come up from Shiloh, Georgia, where he'd worked for fifty cents a week picking tobacco to help support his family. There were eight of them in a two-room shack. The rent was four dollars a month, and that's a lot when you're earning only fifty cents a week.

They'd come North because they got tired of walking a mile and a half for water and having no bathroom.

"But Philadelphia's just as hard," King said. "Bathrooms don't make no difference." Rents were so high, and there was no grass around. He hadn't known about electric lights, either. When his family first arrived here, his mother blew on a light bulb to make it go out.

When I talked about getting out of the ghetto, King said I had no business trying to get him to leave his people, and it was folks like me who kept black people divided. I tried to explain that I wasn't like that, I just felt you owe yourself something. He said he couldn't reason with selfish people like me. We agreed to disagree.

I had such big plans for them. It proved how narrow I really was. How could I expect to move them out of the city when they'd never moved off the corner? I knew that many of my kids had never been to center city; that they had younger brothers and sisters who had never seen a white man except on television. Then I discovered the great government giveaway. When I heard about the funds for a cultural program to take kids to events in town, I got all excited. The intention of the program is really to turn our kids into culture vultures. Some teacher ran a "cultural enrichment program" two years before, when the money was first appropriated. He bought tickets to art shows and chamber-music concerts, and wondered why the kids didn't take advantage of this marvelous opportunity. Then he quit. Five of us who had other ideas for spending the money picked up the mess that had been made of the project and began to have fun. We renamed the program SCENES—each letter stood for something I never could remember—and got a bunch of kids to work with us. We picked three activities a month, which we graded high, medium, and low on our culture scale, bought fifty tickets to each one, and with jazzy bulletin boards, managed to capture the interest of kids who'd never done more in school than throw plates in the lunchroom. For fifty cents, they sat in three-dollar seats at jazz spectaculars, controversial movies, the Ice Capades, and plays on their way to Broadway. For the Supremes concert, there was a ticket line outside my door at seven-thirty in the morning. When we talked up an ice-skating party, even the gang members bought tickets in the belief that we wouldn't steer them wrong. By the time Leontyne Price came to Philadelphia with the Met, the kids were willing to try an opera—that's how much they trusted us.

We called each kid on the phone the night of an affair to remind him of the time and see if we could help with transportation. We gave out points for attending our events and promised a reward for people who accumulated the most points. It was an incredible success. Wherever we went, we had 100 per cent attendance. Wherever we went, we never had an incident that hinted at trouble, or even a show of bad manners. Wherever we went, the kids had a ball. They dressed to the teeth, learned to travel all over the city on public transportation, and even hinted that they'd go places on their own, now that they'd seen how nice it was.

The night we went to see *Streetcar Named Desire*, we had our only tense moment. We filled the first several rows of the theater. None of the kids had ever been to a play before. And they did love it. The problem was that they thought it was a comedy. That ridiculous broad in the white dress guzzling booze and the big dummy in the bowling shirt were the funniest things they'd ever seen. They roared. Through the whole first act. The actors seemed tense. I shrank down in my seat. But how can you be mad? They were beautifully behaved—they just saw the play differently than the rest of the world—which was certainly their privilege. At intermission, I decided something had to be done. In my quietest lecture voice, I talked for fifteen minutes about Tennessee Williams and his pathetic Southern heroines, who, like the slaves, had been devastated by the Civil War and clung to the security of the past. I painted poor Stanley as an animal, reacting only on instinct, trying to survive in an artificial society. They nodded their heads. Poor Blanche. Poor Stella. Poor Stanley. Then the second act began. They roared.

As far as I know, I never got a kid to go farther than twenty minutes from home. But that might not be so bad, if their twenty-minute trips meant as big a change to them as my daily trips to the ghetto meant to me.

I'd lived in Philadelphia all my life, and all I knew about the Black Belt was what I'd read in the paper.

I had hoped that I could find some kind of work that would be exciting, and keep our three-year stay from being a continuation of everything else I'd ever done.

So when I learned that teaching paid three times what Wool-

worth's did, I threw in the towel and joined a program. The Intern teaching program was really tailor-made for me. It's geared to liberal-arts graduates who decide when it's too late that they want to teach. Its premise is a good one: that people who know their subject make better teachers than products of teacher's colleges, who know lots of methods. They put you through an eight-week summer session, the most valuable part of which is practice teaching in summer school; they find you a job; and they promise you a master's degree if you stick with them for thirty credits of night school. I lasted through seventeen, and decided that, although I felt morally obliged to those nice people, I really didn't care about the degree, and just couldn't handle any more of those demoralizing sessions that called themselves ed courses but more closely resembled group therapy. I had the job. And that's all I really wanted.

In spite of the courses, the Intern program is one of the few really well-intended federal projects I know about. The staff is very good—not at all old guard—and they really care about helping you to be a good teacher. The program is geared to the teaching of inner-city kids, and the staff does everything they can to arm you with a sense of humor and an understanding of the kids' problems. They come to visit you in your classroom once a week for two years and act as sounding board and critic. But there's really very little you can be taught about teaching. Imagination, humor, and insight are just not commodities you can buy for $200 a semester. Of the year and a half I spent as an intern, it was that first summer for which I thank them. It gave me a job with all the rights and privileges of a real teacher, put me in touch with real kids and real kids' problems, and gave me a chance to ask lots of questions about what I'd have to deal with in September. It was the blanket I could hang on to while I bit my nails and worried. For that, I'm grateful.

At the end of the summer, I was offered a job at Central High School, a school for supersmart boys where you have to have both a high IQ and a record of achievement to be admitted. Central is a school for people like my brother. Geniuses.

It was a very flattering offer. It was my practice teaching that impressed the people; I was pretty good. But I couldn't stand the idea of teaching the kind of kids I'd grown up with—kids who said and did the right thing because they needed you for a college recommendation. And I guess I couldn't face the possibility of being discovered. My brother was a junior at Central at that time, and he knew lots more bookish stuff than I did. Thirty of him in an English class would destroy me. I mean, I'm smart—I just don't know anything.

For many of the same reasons, I didn't want to teach in the suburbs. I'm a bigot when it comes to overindulged kids. They're too wrapped up in that sequestered world of theirs to understand much about anything. In short, they're culturally deprived.

So, as an avoidance tactic, I requested a job at an all-Negro high school of four thousand, because I'd heard great things about the principal, because city schools pay more, and because I wanted some excitement. I was told to watch out for these kids who'd had babies, attacked teachers, and managed to survive in a world far bigger than mine. They were culturally deprived.

I do believe charity begins at home. I had no hopes of saving kids' souls. I simply wanted to have a good time—too few in our world look forward to Monday mornings. That's why I went to North.

Going for an interview was a scary proposition. I put my hair up for the first time in my life, in the hope that I'd look like a teacher, and wore a skirt that came safely below my knees. It was a twenty-minute drive from center city to the North Philadelphia ghetto area. It would have been an hour by bus and subway. I walked around the school for ten minutes trying to figure out where the main entrance was. The building was gorgeous—it looked so high-schooly. It's a huge stone castle of a place, with turrets and old-fashioned windows. Everyone gripes about the leaky pipes and worn-out floor boards, but I like that dank, old atmosphere. Slick modern schools just don't have any guts, somehow.

I couldn't wait to meet Mr. Butler. I knew little about him, except that in the six months he'd been principal, he'd changed the reputation of the school. He'd replaced policemen with student monitors, collected a bunch of teachers who wanted to try some new methods, and made lots of enemies among the bulwarks of the system. I'd heard that he was appointed as a political gesture, aimed at appeasing the black leaders who were screaming about racial imbalance in the schools. If so, it was just luck that he turned out to be great.

When I met Eli Butler, I was more than impressed. I guess I was in love. He's a dark, massive man who moves with a combination of warmth and authority. He has presence. He asked me why I wanted to work in a school with the highest dropout rate (60 per cent), the highest crime rate, and the highest absentee rate in the city. And wouldn't I have trouble relating to kids whose backgrounds were so different from mine. I didn't know what to say without sounding like a hoodlum myself. I didn't want him to think I got a kick out of the kind of kid that was his biggest problem. So I said nothing except that I liked kids and had a good summer practice teaching at a similar school. I got the job. Probably because he figured I might be better than the next person who walked in off the street.

The first day of school was trauma. It was the noise level that hit me first. The hallways sounded like a football stadium. I went home with the first headache I'd ever had. I had one just like it every day for the next six weeks.

I was struck, too, by the blackness. Being immersed in a Negro world was new to me, and in the dim, artificial light of the corridors, faces seemed to disappear. It struck me funny. I laughed for days.

Then there was the language barrier. It was Christmas before I could understand them without watching mouths.

I wasn't as scared as people said you're supposed to be when you meet your first class. I'm too cocky to expect failure. And I was too excited about meeting the kids to think much about myself.

I talked an awful lot, though I haven't the slightest idea what I said. Something about the course, I guess. And I tried to give them some idea of what they could expect from me, since it's at least as important for kids to know their teacher as their subject. Let's face it: humoring a teacher never hurt anyone.

My opening remarks were a lot better the second year, after I'd decided which ground rules really mattered to me. But for that first class, they weren't too bad. I mean, the kids came back the next day. That means something.

I remember being impressed by the clothes I saw that day. They made me feel shabby. I'd been prepared for a bunch of poverty cases; it was a real shock to face a room full of beautifully dressed students. I puzzled about it until I got to know the kids better, and they told me how their money gets spent. Many of them go South for the summer and pick blueberries for fifty cents a bushel to outfit themselves for school. Lots of them buy clothes on time, and spend months paying off a ten-dollar jacket. And if you've got five or six sisters, you can trade like mad and wear something new every day. If there aren't enough shoes to go around, you take turns going to school. Your grades suffer, but that's certainly preferable to wearing your old lady's sneakers and being embarrassed. That is, if you care about stuff like that. Some kids don't. So there are the well-dressed and the undressed, and very few in between.

I never cared much about clothes. But then, I had an O.K. house to bring friends to, and I was pretty secure about my place in the world. I guess when that security is missing, the image you show the world becomes very important to you. Brendella Harmon once showed me some snapshots of herself taken in her house before a date. There stood Brendella in a handsome dress and matching coat, standing on a bare floor, up to her ankles in trash. There were gaping holes in the wall. Behind her, on one corner of the floor, was a mattress. There were no sheets on it. I realized then how important images really are. I'd never thought of Brendella in any other terms than those befitting her wardrobe. Kenny Murray once said, "Whenever you see some black man in a shiny Cadillac, you can be sure he's got no furniture at home. Man, he probably *sleeps* in that car." And why not. When he drives down the street, he's on top of the world. No one knows what he left behind.

Cheryl was the best-dressed girl in my seventh-period class. That's what made me notice her. She wore the greatest clothes I ever saw, and I was jealous. There were forty students in the class, so it took me a while to get to know much more than her name, but I drew all sorts of conclusions. Like she had to be smart. Anybody with such good taste had to be smart. And I was right.

Not only did she have the brains; she had the skills most of the other kids lack. She wrote beautifully and had great understanding of what she read, and she could spell—my god, she could spell.

She sat in the front row in those great clothes, and did A work, but it took a while to get to know her. She was reserved, in a sophisticated kind of way. And she was absent a lot.

Once we'd begun to talk, I learned all kinds of things about her that just didn't fit. She was a professional go-go girl. Her singing group had made a record, but they couldn't work for a while because one of the girls was pregnant. She was forever being taken to the Youth Study Center for truancy. She lived in three rooms with twenty-one people. She wanted to go to college. She'd never slept in a bed by herself.

I didn't feel like Cheryl's teacher. We were very comfortable together, and we always had lots to chat about. But I saw very little of her. She'd be absent for three weeks at a time, and come back to class with no excuses. The very least I'd learned to expect from truants was a good story. But Cheryl just appeared and did some more beautiful work. By March, she was in danger of failing the year—she'd been absent something like 70 per cent of the term. She said some man at the detention center had gotten interested in her and promised her a scholarship to college if she'd just attend school. I got all excited and talked up the "good life" that education affords. With every word, I got more enthused about Cheryl in college, and out of the slums, and the people she'd meet. The more I talked, the better the world got. I don't know how she reacted, but I sure was convinced. SCENES was sponsoring a trip to Dr. Zhivago that night, and Cheryl had bought a ticket. So I suggested that she come home with me after school, and I'd take her to Penn to see a class and look around. Then she could have dinner with us, and we'd meet the other kids at the movie. It would be great. She said O.K., if her mother would let her. I dashed to a phone. Her mother said it was nice of me, and my, I had a lovely voice. It was settled.

The afternoon was lots of fun. We walked all around the university, and I introduced Cheryl to some of our friends there. We had a roast for dinner, and though she must have felt a little weird eating with us, she carried it off well—very quietly, but well. She didn't say

much about our apartment, which is really quite spectacular—a huge living room with a cathedral ceiling, lots of sunshine, great shaggy rugs, a fireplace, fresh flowers—but she did mention that she liked the floors. They were so shiny, and there weren't any rotten places.

We went to the movie, and I lost her in the mob of kids. I felt all glowy. It was good for her to get a look at someone else's life. Even if she wasn't wild about it, at least she'd know it exists.

When the movie was over, we dropped Cheryl and some of the others at a bus stop. Cheryl thanked me for dinner and said good night. That was the last time I ever saw her.

You've gotta get yourself together, is what the kids are always saying. I couldn't manage it, and that's why I botched up so much that first year, I was as self-centered as the teen-agers I was supposed to be helping. The outside things—mounds of clerical work, record keeping, lesson plans—had to be handled, and that left little time for inside things. I didn't really understand my position in the class. I did not understand a great deal of what I was doing or why I was doing it.

I was frantic about preparing for five classes a day, marking hundreds of papers a week, dealing with the records of forty home-room charges, and making the best of such demoralizing duties as hall patrol, which makes you a sort of rent-a-cop. Since I couldn't learn to challenge the ready reasons every kid had for roaming the corridors, and felt it was somehow better to accept their stories than accuse them of lying, I was a poor patroller. Making the best of things entailed hiding in the toilet, till the vice principal in charge of checking checked me out.

I didn't begin to know what to teach; my own need for organization and purpose hung me up as much as the school's limitations of books and supplies. In math or history, there's an inherent sequence to fall back on; in English there's the whole world. Challenging, yes—but far more frustrating to a newcomer who didn't know what a lesson plan was and couldn't work the mimeograph. There was no logical place to begin. The kids couldn't read, and I wasn't a reading teacher. They didn't speak my language, but I was damned if I'd presume to suggest that theirs was wrong. Hell—they communicated at least as successfully as I did, and that's what language is for, isn't it?

So what was I doing there? The first day of school taught me that I could not hope to have any fun with two hundred empty faces. Mischief would have been exciting; hostility challenging; but apathy was unendurable. I don't think I thought much about doing anything for the kids—I simply had to find some way of sparking my days. What happened inside the kids was a by-product.

The fashionable topic of teachers' meetings was "Let's Make Learning Fun"—which wasn't a bad idea. It's certainly preferable to making learning agony. I saw lots of inspired, missionary types playing with tape recorders and finger paints; they gloated because the kids were Relating and Socializing and Coming to Class. But the whole technique bothered me, somehow. I mean, you can't just play around when kids can't read a want ad in a newspaper. Making learning fun is a great premise, as long as learning is taking place. More often than not, it isn't.

The old-guard teachers throw up walls with their lectures and mickey-mouse assignments, and the kids turn them off. The experimentalists spend so much time Reaching the kids that little substance is ever conveyed. These dedicated souls understand the kids to death—and their classes play them to the hilt.

Teachers seem to assume that they play the starring role in the kids' lives. What rubbish that is. To many of the kids, school doesn't even exist, except as a place where you've got to go to stay out of trouble. Or to get warm. Or to pick up girls.

In my forty-five minutes a day with each class, I had the feeling I could accomplish more if I could provide something they couldn't get out on the street—skills and ideas. It was a meager philosophy to begin with, but it provided some modicum of direction for me. So I muddled along with the business of getting through each day's lesson, and pink forms, yellow forms, white forms, green forms, and the problems of manipulating two hundred kids, and the incredible job of sorting out my own ideas and putting them to work.

I found that I was forced to spend a disproportionate amount of time worrying about things like grades. Four times a year, I was handed huge IBM sheets and told to fill them in with a number-two pencil. They make everything look so ordered, which is ridiculous, because everything's such a mess when it comes to grades. For one thing, they make subjective judgments look foolishly arbitrary. Even if I had given scores of objective tests, my records would show only the kids' test-taking ability, which is lousy. If you look at their IQ scores, 90 per cent of them have slid down about 30 points since they were six. What you have is a record of their inability to read—nothing more. Besides the inaccuracy of the test grades, classroom behavior and attendance have to play a role in grading. Such things are never really factors in suburban schools, because kids come—it's that simple. But what do you do with a kid who shows up once a week and does great work? I'm pretty sure I do more harm than good by failing a kid—it's his anticipation of failure that keeps ego too low to work with. You never know whether your F will be the one that makes a kid drop out of school—and who can live with that? By the same token, when the demands are minimal, like "Come to class," passing a kid who fails to meet them makes a mockery of those who do, and destroys the few standards you attempt to establish.

What a hassle. It's worse with a senior. He's stuck it out for so long in a system that's done almost nothing for him that you just don't want to give him any more aggravation.

I told Millard Atkins a thousand times that he'd have to put his face in the place if he wanted to pass. And to please do it for me, if not for himself—I couldn't stand the thought of flunking a senior. A thousand times, he turned on his gorgeous smile, and told me he'd shape up, and used that particular tone of voice that made me feel very feminine. He continued to skip my class.

Eight o'clock classes really were trying, especially when it was cold and wet and dark outside. But I always figured if I could make it, the kids could. It was my dollar, but their grade. So day after day I crawled out of bed and into school, and as the winter droned on, I grew jealous of Millard Atkins all cozy and warm while I was suffering.

Charles Zern was another one. And since I hadn't had such long, lovely chats with him, I could flunk him easily and forget it. Millard's name was at the top of my roll sheet (right over Phinorice Bermudez) and Charles's was at the bottom. They made a solid border of zeroes that trimmed the page.

Graduation time approached, and it became evident that my two cutters were not going to join their class in the ceremonies. I felt awful; but they had hung themselves.

One evening in May, I saw Charles Zern walking in center city. I wouldn't have known him if he hadn't said hello. I asked him how come he was downtown, and he said he worked at a restaurant till 2 A.M.

"But that's ridiculous," I said. "No wonder you can't make an eight o'clock class. Do you need money that badly?" He was embarrassed. He explained to his feet that his father was in Vietnam and his mother was on the critical list in the hospital. He had to work at night to support the kids, and he had to get them to school in the morning. So it was kind of hard to get to my class. It was kind of hard.

I hate to find out about kids' problems. It spoils any ideas I may have about making T. S. Eliot an important part of their lives. Kids produce only if you demand it of them. Yet, knowing, how can I make any demands of them? How can I not? I would be just another crumb, in a long line of crumbs, who would let them slip out of school not knowing how to read. So I push. And I spend a lot of time forgetting the stuff that hurts.

Charles caught me off guard. There was no time for forgetting. Grades had to be entered for the year. I passed him, of course. His mother was still in the hospital, and his father was still in the war, but his little brother came to watch Charles get his diploma. He was the first person in his whole family to graduate from high school.

Millard Atkins didn't get his diploma. He came to school one day the next fall to say hi and tell me he was playing drums with a big band at the Uptown Theater. Rob and I went to hear him and clapped like crazy.

I've probably had serious grading problems with half my kids. And though I try to look like one-who-knows, I always wind up feeling stupid about the whole system.

Harriet Martin walked in after a five-week tour of duty somewhere and asked if she was passing for the year. After five weeks and no excuse. I was very obnoxious about it all, and I rather resented having been ignored. So I took the easy way out and talked teacher to her. Things like, "Your job is school, and you've walked out on it." And "Am I supposed to give grades, or are you supposed to earn them?" When I finally shut up, she told me her four-year-old son had been hit by a car and she'd been at the hospital for weeks. Now he was home, but the cast was on his whole body, and he had to be fed and carried like an infant. Note: If you start with a question instead of a lecture, you save yourself a lot of embarrassment. So there I was, talking to someone's mother about what her job was. The teacher. With big problems like grades.

I guess little was really accomplished in any area that first year. But I learned to ask some of the important questions about what I should do and how I should do it. I even learned a few of the answers—nothing grand, but enough for an opener.

The Establishment has been failing for years. I guess that's why I never worried much about doing the "right thing." However, since it

seemed that learning is the thing that should happen in school, the situations that are the most conducive to learning require that certain proprieties be maintained. Kids can't learn when they're walking around the room to chat with friends; they can't learn when their teacher spends all her time disciplining a couple of troublemakers. They can learn, however, when they're sitting in seats of their own choice; or when they're wearing sunglasses; or when their teacher smiles. They can even learn when they're chewing gum! Except when they crack it. Because then I can't teach. So the rules made themselves

It's so easy to ignore the obvious—it was right in front of my nose. The issue was reading.

> HEARS HOW I fEEL ABOUT REAdING
> I LiKe to ReAd bECAUSE if you
> couldNt REAd you might AS weLL hAVE
> No Life

The kids I grew up with never seemed to care much about learning. They talked a lot about grades, but the learning itself was simply a consequence of the mechanics of their lives. The people I teach, though, are quite literally fighting for their education. More often than not they come from bookless homes. They are pressured to stay out of school—by their own desires for clothes and radios, and often by the need to provide a substantial portion of the family income. For many, their very presence in the classroom is a triumph.

> But you Know I Know what most people
> donot Know about. But you Know for
> a fact that some of the kids who do
> go to school it its not there fult.
> There are some graw ups who keep their
> kids out of school. because they don't believe
> in school

I can't begin to imagine the problems that illiterate parents impose on a child's development. I do know that I read and wrote at home with my parents long before I went to school—and I wasn't really ahead of the game as a result of it. But many of my students had never seen a book when they entered school, and they spent the first semester learning to use the toilet.

Contact with the kids' parents is nearly impossible. They never manage to show up at school functions or parents' night. Many of them hold two jobs and manage a brood of young ones. Others resent our white Establishment—or are afraid of it. I get only occasional glimpses:

Dear Teacher
Why alton was absent sep 28. and 29, he hurt his leg in school running.

mrs Bride

From Sarah Mother
Friday 28 Sarah feet was sore she couldn't wear her shoes

Beuleah.

I am always surprised by my kids' outspoken concern with education—be it a prerequisite for jobs or a status symbol. "White kids get homework every night—*that's* why I want it."

They are startlingly honest about their deficiencies. Their pleas for help are not at all in keeping with their flawless cool—their tough-guy façades.

> I like reading but I have to use my finger
> Otherwise the lines run together. Sometimes
> when I read my eyes get watery. So I
> don't raise my hand to read, I wait until
> I'm called on. And ther reason is because
> I don't understand what I read.

> The thing I hate most about myself
> is the way I spell.

I'm always yelling that brains and skills don't necessarily correlate. But these kids have failed for so long that it's impossible to convince them that they need only the skills—reading and writing—to be able to prove their brains. They're so defensive, and so defeated.

> If I could be reborn or changed in
> any way I would rather be the
> same as I am now, but, with a
> little bit more intelligents. I feel
> as thought I don't have enought
> intelligents. If every body had enought
> intelligent It would be a better world.

Lots of kids who are virtually nonreaders walk around with a knife in one pocket and a dictionary in the other. They play their roles relentlessly.

like to give the play called Romia + juliten. I would That one of my favortie plays.

Reading is, I'm convinced, the core of more problems than Congress could cope with in a decade. And when the cries make themselves heard, they're deafening.

I like books BECusS they'ne the only things that dont tell you you'Re stupid

But where do you begin? Certainly not in the book room. If a seventeen-year-old is going to face all the frustrations of learning to read, and plug through a book that goes yah-yah at all his inadequacies, he's got to have a pretty good reason for suffering through it. Maybe that's what they mean by motivation. Somehow, a kid has to feel it's important to read. He's either got to want to or need to.

When the biology classes were tested, it was discovered that more than 90 per cent of the kids couldn't read the textbook they'd been using for six months. The tenth-graders I taught have an average reading level of second grade. Handing them a high school text means no one will read at all. Not only is it too frustrating, it just isn't worth it. I mean, how many ghetto kids can get turned on to *Jane Eyre?* By the same token, you can't demoralize them by going back to Spot and Puff. So you have to find something with a high interest level written in simple vocabulary. *Nigger. West Side Story. Raisin in the Sun.* There's even some money around for such purchases. Never enough, of course. What we need is five dollars a year for each kid. We could buy him a collection of paperbacks which he could keep. With a few books in the house, whole families might start reading; the kids could be the big shots who help their parents.

But that's too much to hope for. At best, some stodgy department head begrudges you fifteen dollars for a set of paperbacks that must survive the back pockets of four or five kids. And if that department head is Adolf Farber, *Raisin in the Sun* is too controversial, so you have to go to Mr. Butler, who buys it for you, thus making Adolf Farber your enemy.

One of the problems of being a first-year teacher was that I was intimidated by my department head and lived in fear of his unannounced visits to my class. His comments on my teaching were restricted to searing remarks about the smudged blackboards, the uneven window shades, and the stinking gym suits I let kids leave in my closet.

Having been berated for not decorating the bulletin boards in my room, and realizing that I was simply not the bulletin-board type, I had asked the kids to take care of it and keep me out of trouble. They'd done a valiant job, but Adolf Farber seemed unimpressed.

I taught very hard as he sat in the back of the room looking around. It wasn't a bad lesson, either. But just as I was getting to the clincher question, Mr. Farber bolted out of his seat, strode to the front of the class, and ripped a large poster off the wall. The kids were as startled as I.

"What do we have here?" he asked me.

"We have a poster that Reginald Thompson made," I ventured.

"Don't you notice anything unusual about it?"

I noticed that it was colorful; that the slogan under the picture he'd drawn proclaimed rather cleverly the rewards of staying in school; that the poster represented more hours of work than anything Reginald had done all year. He wasn't too good at English, but he was an artist; this had been his chance to show me he cared. But I was too upset by the redness I felt in my face to volunteer any more information. The kids always made a big fuss when I blush. It's one of the few talents I have that they lack.

"There's a misspelled word on this."

Farber was incredulous. He was horrified.

"We don't hang up mistakes here at North."

He dumped the poster in the wastebasket and left.

The class sat silent, trying not to stare at me and make everything worse. I didn't know what to do first. I wanted to save face; to get revenge; to understand if I'd really done something horrid. I was certainly not going to let Reginald's efforts sit in the wastebasket. You just don't do that to a kid who's attempted something for you. I tacked the poster back on the wall. Then I faced the class and tried to pick up some shred of my ruined lesson.

It took most of the year for me to learn how to handle Farber. Once I began to talk back to him, he left me alone. But he gave me a C rating for the year. The irony of it was that I really was a C teacher—I hadn't learned to do much more than talk to the kids. But Farber's grade meant something else. For that, I resented it.

When I managed to get a decent book to give my classes, I didn't have much trouble getting them to read it. I'm enough of a dramatist to work up some interest. Sustaining it, though, is more difficult. You've got to be resourceful enough to vary activities without turning the class into a circus. And there's got to be a point. You have to be able to articulate what was taught, regardless of the way you taught it. A discussion has to be more than that; a story can't be just plot.

Stephanie Barns always gave the impression that she was a great authority on teaching. She's just a couple of years older than I, but she wears grownup clothes and enunciates a little too clearly. The kids hate her, but she doesn't know it. She just walks around in her ramrod posture and her Bonwit's seventh-floor dresses, using her crystalline voice to proclaim herself the last word on any given subject. Her classes spent weeks building a model Shakespearean theater, and Stephanie unveiled it with great pride at a faculty meeting. The faculty applauded, and I couldn't help feeling, So what? For weeks, the project provided her with a ready-made lesson plan; she certainly had something to show for herself. But what value does a damn cardboard theater have for kids who can't read? I get all wrought up inside thinking about the amount of time schools waste. We probably lose three hours a day just changing classes, serving lunch, and wading through clerical procedures like roll taking. To screw up what little class time is left is disgusting.

I've begun to feel that among the superstraight, ultra-middle-class

Negroes like Stephanie, there is a strong resentment of the kids, as though the kids reflect badly on them. They always seem to be denying that our clientele is different from any other school's.

More than other teachers, they seem preoccupied with monkey business like how a kid sits, what he wears, and whether he raises his hand.

It's teachers like Stephanie Barns who, for all their proclaimed expertise, convinced me that a cultural gap is a far greater liability than a racial difference in dealing with our kids.

I was paired with her in Room 504. Although the school operates on three overlapping shifts to alleviate the population problem, there's a portion of the day when everyone's in the building and there just aren't enough classrooms. So the geniuses in the roster office scheduled two classes together in the barnlike 504. What they expected two teachers to do with eighty-five kids, I don't know. Showing movies is a fine idea once in a while, but when you're there five days a week and no movies have been ordered and there are no shades on those ten-foot windows anyway, you have to come up with another idea.

I knew enough, even as a beginner, to realize that once a discipline problem has been created, there's little hope of ever being anything but a policeman. But to avoid the problem from the outset involves incredibly tight structuring and planning. You've got a lot working against you. For one thing, you can't learn eighty-five names for a while, and the anonymity the kids have affords them a chance to make trouble without getting in trouble. You can't give out books, because there aren't more than forty copies of any one text in school. There musn't be any extensive writing, either. Room 504 has no desks—only chairs lined up on risers. To write, you need a book to lean on; and since most of the kids don't carry books, it's a lost cause.

I asked Stephanie if she'd teach the first week. I was at a loss as to where to begin with such a group, and I was very in awe of my partner, who'd intimidated me with her talk of creative dramatics, teaching Shakespeare, and the advantages of being black in dealing with the kids at North. She has incredible energy, and as she strode around in Those Clothes and talked of the myriad activities her classes were working on, I felt more than ever like a pimply-faced kid with a droopy lower lip. She was a lady, and an expert at her job; my dislike for her had to be nothing more than jealousy.

She agreed to teach, since she had stacks of some magazine with a play in it she'd been wanting to try. I was relieved; I didn't have to expose myself for a week, and I could pick up lots of pointers from her in the meantime.

The kids clattered in, seeing to it that they wasted a good fifteen minutes getting seated. Stephanie didn't say anything about the noise—I guessed she expected them to quiet down when she introduced the play. I was wrong. There was no introduction at all. She handed out the magazines, assigned parts randomly, and began to read the narrator's line. Wait a minute! You can't do that—a kid has to know what he's about—he has to have a reason to read; he has to be motivated to want to read. The noise level increased. Stephanie seemed oblivious. She continued to plow through her part, as kids tossed cigarettes to each other and joked about last night's party. Only the kids who'd been given roles were attentive—or were they scared? No one finds it easy to perform in front of a large group, and these actors hadn't even had a chance to read over their lines. Maybe they wouldn't know the words. Maybe they'd be laughed at. What was she saying, anyway?

It was a shocker of a week. No, it was only three days. By Wednesday, Stephanie told me she'd finished the play and it was my turn. I ventured a question about follow-up activities—discussions, quizzes, or any related project that would make the play meaningful, and involve the kids who hadn't yet done anything but make trouble. No, dramatizing it was sufficient. The play was finished. I was annoyed. That halting, expressionless reading was her conception of dramatization. The fact that three-quarters of the class had never opened the magazine didn't faze her. She didn't even have any trouble looking me in the eye when, at lunch that day, she delivered a soliloquy on effective teaching.

I understood why the kids hated her. She'd never really spoken to them in three days. There was no attempt made to learn their names, or see to it that they did any work, or find out what they thought. She was a teacher of English—not of people. And her teaching was unquestionably lousy. The aura of superiority she created lasted about five minutes with the kids. Only suckers like me had failed to see through the veneer.

I couldn't wait to plan my lesson. I'd show her.

That night I wrote a list: Never trust a cop. All Jews are stingy. Negroes are inferior to whites. Teachers play favorites. Irishmen drink too much. Teen-age marriages don't last. Ten or fifteen juicy items. I mimeographed a sheet of open-ended sentences like, "The thing that makes me different from my friends is ——." That was designed as both an interest grabber (everyone likes to write about himself) and a sneaky way of getting the kids to discover that they describe themselves by their differences—not their similarities. I wrote out a bunch of questions and statements designed to make me look dumb, so the kids would do the teaching.

It wasn't hard to see to it that I was the first one in class—the kids had already decided there was no need to hurry, so they stopped off in the bathroom for a smoke or in the cafeteria for a sweet before they ambled to 504. I met them at the door with the mimeographed sheet and a big grin.

"Betcha can't do this in ten minutes," I said.

And because the sheet looked like fun and the challenge looked easy, they grabbed chairs and began to write. Newcomers arrived and were struck by the silence in the room. I didn't even have to be cute for them—they simply followed their classmates' example and got to work.

There was more than ten minutes' worth of statements on the paper, and I interrupted them before they'd had time to finish, just so they'd know I wasn't playing around. In the meantime, I'd plastered the blackboard with my list of stereotypes, and they were intrigued enough to keep quiet and listen. What did the papers they'd written about themselves have to do with the ruthless blasphemies on the board? What was this screwy lady up to anyway?

I began with a question: "Which of these statements are true and which are false?"

We went through the list. Then I asked about exceptions to the rule—had anyone ever met a nice cop? A fair teacher? What does this prove?

And take a look at those sheets you wrote. Did you describe yourself in terms of how you were *like* others, or how you're different from them? Oh, yeah. . . .

I hoped Stephanie Barns's brain was farther from her paper work than her flat little nose. It was killing not to be able to grab her by the shoulders and tell her how great I was.

By the end of the period, the kids had decided that if you can find one teen-age marriage that sticks or one sober Irishman, the stereotype falls apart. And where do people get off saying Negroes are inferior? They'd learned.

"What?" I asked, by way of summary.

"That you can't talk about all people like one," a girl said.

I was delighted.

"Except," she added. "Except Jews. Everyone knows all Jews are stingy."

The bell rang.

The ed courses I found so offensive were always stressing the mechanics of writing lesson plans. You've got to have an aim, which you print at the top of the page. Then your activities, designed to arrive at the aim at the lesson's end. It all sounded so pedantic—I was too cool to bother with that kind of stuff.

It took about a month of blundering before I gave in and wrote a real lesson plan. Funny, how the discipline of stating your ways and means on paper forces you to really teach. And if you've written it all out, you can step back and look at it before show time, to see exactly what's going on. That's where you can really save a lesson. There's got to be a balance between how much teacher talks, how much kids work alone, and how much interaction there is.

I'm a talker. It's so easy to rattle on, making terribly important points, and so easy to forget that kids will give you about ten minutes of that kind of self-indulgence before they shut you off. They've got to be involved. I could have told them in a second what a stereotype

is and why it's used and what's wrong with it. But telling doesn't mean a damn thing, unless you're teaching kids who take notes and listen to lectures. They've got to discover their own truth, if it's to be a part of them.

But there are some points you just can't make. When I taught poetry, I talked about the sounds of words, and how some are hard, like hissing, and some are soft and round, like wallow.

"Look at a word like flower," I said. "It's not in the same class with buzz or whack, but it's full, like a blossom."

Dwaine Bulford sat in the back of the room looking devilish.

"Try hibiscus," he said.

Some kids are too smart for their own good.

Others are hard to convince for different reasons. They're a well-indoctrinated product of a superstitious culture that has an answer for everything. You can't fight mysticism. I learned that and much more from Christabelle Sands.

Kids very rarely laugh lovingly at someone. They are the cruelest kind of people. That's why I was amazed at their treatment of Chrissy. Everyone laughs at her—but they adore her.

Chrissy was a recent immigrant from a Georgia farm. She was one of nine children. Her dialect was almost unintelligible. She was built like I'd like to be. She was, in a very quiet way, the most delightful person I'd ever known. She rarely spoke, but when she got excited, something wild happened inside her, and torrents of ideas and opinions came raging out. That's when we'd laugh. She said bagogogy instead of biology, and imbication instead of education. I guess the kids liked her because she wasn't at all an oddball, she was very friendly, and she danced great. She just talked funny.

Her favorite subject was John Kennedy. She would have died for him willingly. When we discussed prejudice and stereotypes, Chrissy announced that she hated Catholics. Seizing an opportunity to make my lesson meaningful, I said, "But President Kennedy was a Catholic."

"He was not," she announced. "You cain burlieve evythin' you read."

The kids laughed, but Chrissy knew. The subject was closed.

I learned a lot from her. Like if you want to make money, you sleep on an empty vanilla bottle. It makes you dream of someone who's dead. Then you call someone in the deceased's family on the phone. They give you three numbers. You bet on those numbers, and you always win. It's that simple.

My husband visited me at school one day, and the kids lost no time in engaging him in conversation. They're always amazed to discover that their teacher has an "other life." They seem to think we get locked up in closets at night and let out in the morning. They stared at him like mad, and asked questions furiously. At one point, he had occasion to answer Christabelle, and he addressed her by name. The next day, she began to talk about him.

"He's so nice," she said. "I can tell he don't beat you. And he's wise—he talks jest like Kennedy." A big breath. "And when he said my name, I liked to *die!*"

He'd said her name. He'd made her a person.

Because she couldn't stand the uncertainty surrounding the assassination, and because of Johnson's inability to relate to his public, Chrissy launched a hate campaign, based on the premise that Johnson killed Kennedy. Admittedly, the contrast between the two is a big comedown. Like most of us, Chrissy found the man's sparerib style offensive. She talked about Leecy Bird and Lacy Bird with teeth-grinding vengeance and spent lots of time discussing the wedding: "Who else spends all that money on a dress you never wear but once—and it were even ugly." And the presidential beagles: "Dem dogs eat better'n I do!"

After a heated discussion on Vietnam, Chrissy was prompted to write a letter to Johnson. It was the first letter she'd ever written, and she had a lot of trouble finding out where to buy a stamp. She waited three months for an answer. None came.

Sometime later in the term, I got a curt note: Christabelle Sands has been transferred to a speech class. Please drop her from your roll.

I was miserable. I'd miss her terribly, and I had the feeling that her speech was part of her charm and no one had any business tampering with charm.

She said a mushy farewell at our last class, and I asked her if our talks had helped her to form any new political opinions.

"Yes'm," she said. "I hates Johnson so much now, I won't even buy the wax!"

So I lost Chrissy to a speech class. The special reading program pulled out several of my other charges. But I didn't feel so bad in those cases. The reading teachers, though by no means human dynamos, did accomplish a lot. The problem was, they took only the worst cases—the nonreaders—and left the "average" student (a mess by any other standard) to plod along in a huge class with a teacher unskilled in reading techniques. The nonreaders really learned, and in a few months they'd be into fourth-grade books. They'd stop cutting classes, and would walk around looking very cocky. But the bulk of the school population continued to be bogged down by sheer numbers. It was the scale of the problem that defeated you. No matter how successful a pilot program was, it touched no more than a tiny slice of the school.

What they really have to do is change our concept of elementary school, and get rid of those cutesy, cheerleader-type girls who play cut-and-paste with the kids. If we flooded the primary grades with competent professionals, kids would learn to read. It's that simple. It really is.

William Jones, charming and well-spoken, was president of the senior class. He couldn't read or write. He took his exams orally. The only aggravation he had all year was from our Mr. Farber. "No senior can graduate from high school until he can read and write."

Which was fine. I couldn't have agreed more. But wasn't it a little late? To keep William from graduating would certainly do more damage than good. The class would lose a leader; the leader would fall into disgrace. If, by some remote chance, we could learn from the Jones experience, there would be a great revolution in the school system.

Isn't it Russia that reveres teachers? I heard that somewhere. It's strange that so little prestige is associated with teaching in America. Being an educator ought to mean a huge responsibility and a great talent. But teachers are just a bunch of laborers. And they've done as much as anyone to earn that status, I guess. Other professions have bar exams and graduate schools and internships. There's much big talk about similar requirements for teachers, but they really amount to nothing more than putting in time. There just aren't any standards. Promotions are based on seniority, so ability goes unrecognized.

For all the jerks running around, North has an awful lot of top-notch people—maybe a fifth of the two hundred on the staff, many more than in the poshy suburban school that graduated me six years ago. Butler attracts them like a magnet.

A kid could get a first-rate education at North, if he hit the right people and didn't get smothered by the size of his classes. But it was a special kind of education, for a special kind of student. Ghetto children don't necessarily buy the idea of education as an end in itself. While middle-class kids learn what's dished out to them, our kids had to be cajoled into learning. Since standard institutional techniques just don't work with potential dropouts, classrooms at North often looked more like a circus. Hours of precious time were spent in simply grabbing interest. And though the games we played made real teaching possible, they rendered our school irrelevant to academically oriented students, willing to cover more ground, with fewer frills.

People accused Butler of running the school like a kindergarten. Teachers couldn't get to him, because his office was always full of kids. Every student was an exception to the rule in his eyes, so it was hard for any teacher to discipline a kid without Butler's intervening. That's how he made enemies. Teachers would scream that they weren't safe in the building—that the kids got away with murder. They had a point. But the success that Butler's had in building morale and raising the aspiration level of our kids meant a lot more to me than the maintenance of order for order's sake.

When Cecil Moore, a flashy Negro lawyer, was running for mayor, the city was a racial hotbed. Rumor had it that Cecil was bringing Dick Gregory to North for a rally in the schoolyard. They were going to call the kids out of the building with loudspeakers. The school was full of cops, and everyone was very psyched-up. At twelve-thirty, a half-hour before the scheduled rally, Mr. Butler got on the loud-speaker.

"I understand Mr. Moore and some of his friends are planning to pay us a visit," he began. "I think we ought to go out and hear what the gentlemen have to say."

Then he outlined a procedure for leaving the building. Teachers were livid. How dare he dismiss school and give in to those trouble-makers? How dare he put teachers into a mob situation that could turn into a riot? Where was all this going to end?

It ended an hour after it began. We stood in the rain and listened to Cecil and Gregory talk about black schools for black students, and black government for black citizenry. They screamed and carried on about twentieth-century slavery, and the kids ate it up. There was lots of cheering, and a few kids I didn't know made some nasty cracks to me. I tried awfully hard to learn something—to understand the rationale of statements like, "You can't learn in that building, so you've got to burn it down." I was terribly disillusioned. I'd been a Dick Gregory fan for years. Had Butler not suggested that we move outdoors, I might even have walked out with the kids, just to hear him. But what I heard wasn't the bright young spokesman I'd seen on TV. He was a black man inciting black kids to destroy a system he wasn't prepared to replace. He was hostile and unreasoning. He was an ass.

The rally lasted for an hour. Then Mr. Butler took the mike and thanked the gentlemen for sharing their ideas with our students.

"Now, I think it's time to get out of the rain and go back to class," he said.

It was that easy. The kids stopped making angry sounds and began to make kid sounds. In ten minutes, classes were in session.

Butler was the man of the hour. I suppose things could have backfired. Teachers could have been pushed around. The rally could have turned into a riot. But none of that happened. Butler's critics hated him more for proving them wrong in their prophecies. His fans lauded him more. He may just turn out to be famous one day. It won't surprise me at all.

Watching Eli Butler deal with the powers—white and black—without becoming an Uncle Tom, is exciting. He somehow manages to use each incident that arises with the press, the school board, the faculty, and the students to prove himself and to win them over. He builds his reputation meticulously. His is the studied, deliberate progression of an important man.

He promised the kids a new cafeteria—and got it for them. He reinstituted the school dances that had been labeled "too dangerous to risk." He got $80,000 worth of scholarships to be divied up among seniors. He stayed at his desk from seven A.M. till five P.M. with parents and problems, trying to hang on to every kid on roll.

When he is working with the kids, though, he meets his hardest challenges. You can't expect a school with a dropout rate of more than half to suddenly graduate everyone who enters, just because you're being inspiring.

One of the things that annoyed me most about the kids was their aspiration level. If you asked them to daydream about what they'd be if the world were theirs, they'd say a secretary. Or a mechanic. It takes a hell of a lot to kill a dream, and there's nothing more horrible than a man without one. Especially when he's fourteen.

I pictured my future being nothing because I am nothing.

I have FAIL with help
I also FAIL trying by myself
FAilure is like shame

I am a failure
I was born as a failure
But I guess that's life

I picture my future being a lonesome house.

I have always been
told, whenever failing try again
is faith so easy to keep

What's the big deal about staying in school anyway, unless you can read and write and reason better as a result? A diploma makes some difference when you go for a job, I guess. But it represents little more than endurance for our kids. They've made it, when so many others have failed. They're hard put to tell you what it means in terms of education. Our graduates read, on the average, at sixth-grade level; they can neither speak nor write standard English. But they've put in twelve years. And what they've got to show for it is a diploma. It's especially nauseating when you realize how easily they could have been taught. They're a captive audience, and they want to achieve.

But it's easier to throw up your hands at the scale of the problem before you and rationalize your days away behind an official roll book and an outdated curriculum that just doesn't work.

The average kid is almost doomed to be forgotten in a school of four thousand. And even if you take an interest, there's little you can do for one in a class of forty. In terms of the kids' needs, it's just horrible how little you can do.

Everyone hated Ethel Calowell. It was why she was there—to be hated. She was big, and ugly, and the first day of school she pushed me into a desk and ruined eighty-two cents' worth of stocking. She was so mean she made my mouth water.

She sat in the back of the room and read cheapy magazines and cracked gum. Her thighs hung out under her skirt, and her great, huge legs supported themselves in thick, filthy socks. There was no girl in Ethel.

She was not the sort you said hi to. You didn't say anything, really; except, "For God's sake, Ethel, crack your gum *quietly!*" For three months she did nothing but present her body daily and expose her thighs. I finally said, "Look, Ethel, you obviously can't pass if you don't work—that's your choice. But I won't bug you about it as long as you don't impose your things on me." She didn't say a word. But I never again heard her gum. It was a comfortable arrangement.

Some time after Thanksgiving, Ethel turned in a composition. She got a C+ on it. Things didn't change much after that. Except that she said something very severe, very apt, to a dumb kid across the aisle and I laughed—which united us, of course, in an unspoken understanding that we knew who was cool (us) and who was jive (the dumb kid). After that she changed her seat to the front row—

smack in the middle. I decided it was a kind of insurance—if she should smile at me, no one could see it.

When we read poetry, Ethel brought more cheapy books to class, which was O.K. Somehow, the fact that she came, relentlessly, moved me. She didn't *have* to come—there were only stray relatives at home to account for her, and they wanted her to work instead of freeload. Once when she was particularly belligerent I asked her why she bothered coming to school. "It's warmer than outside," she said. "I'll stay till April."

But it was a rainy spring, and when I started a project on Japanese haiku, Ethel wrote,

> I grab for my life
> Though death is not far away
> I died when I was born

And all I could do was give her a grade.

The Second Year

The Shell
Inside the dark house in the Middle of the road
all I hear is foot step back and forth.
They don't stop to see if I'm sick or hungry.
They don't know if I'm there or gone.
I watch them as they go past with their head turn up in the air
I ask myself What is wrong?
What have I done? And all I hear is
Be what you are and not what they want you to Be.
By William

F UNNY HOW William and I were learning the same thing. I felt it
from the first day of the second year. Once the madness of the first
year was over, you could sit back just a little and look at things. Your
scope was still narrow, but it was possible to get a picture of you and
them and to watch the interaction.

The biggest difference between the first year and the second was
that I was really beginning to teach now. Part of the change in me
was simply that I'd learned to shut up. My lessons were less enter-
taining, of course—I didn't rant and rave so much. But the kids were
learning more since I'd learned to keep them active. I was catching
on to the difference between feeding them material and motivating

48

them to seek it themselves. They seemed to be working more independently—and they seemed to be working. It was the greatest.

I'd learned to keep quiet in the face of problems, too. I didn't feel compelled to solve their troubles—no stranger ever solved mine. The kids seemed just as happy and open. I guess all they wanted was an ear.

"I have no place to stay. I couldn't do my homework in the subway; the light wasn't no good."

"Please excuse me for last week. I went down South to some funerals. My uncle killed his wife and baby and then hisself. I liked it in the country. It was different."

"I think I'm pregnant because I spit up some again this morning. But maybe it was the hot dogs and gravy on the rice. This food ain't even what I'd feed my cat. It gets you if you're pregnant."

"Do you ever wonder what it's like? Being me, I mean? I think about it a lot. When my father use me, I cry. I can't tell my mother, she be mad at that."

There is nothing easier than being yourself. Which is why, if you play it right, teaching is such a joy. It's a tactic that occasionally proves disastrous, but on the whole, anything's better than being a phony. Grownups I knew as a kid were always so busy role-playing that they didn't seem to be people. They were parent types, teacher types, and so on. It's incredible that no amount of failure in handling their charges prompted them to try any new tactics. Like honesty, for instance. It was a cardinal sin for my parents to say, "Gee, I just don't know"; or for my teachers to say, "I was wrong—I feel like a heel." They felt it incumbent upon themselves to be the last word. And because they weren't, their answers were pat answers, empty answers. Grownups had scripts that they'd memorized, consisting of phrases like when-you're-older-you'll-change-your-mind. They gave orders: Wear your boots; raise your hand; for God's sake remember to flush the toilet. For all their talk about manners, they never really thought it necessary to treat us with common courtesy. Grownups don't respect children. I might have been cute, talented, or precocious, but I was a curio to adults—not a person.

I'm very bitter about the whole thing. And I nurture my hostility. I want to remember every injustice I suffered, so that maybe I can avoid growing up to be a grownup. There are better things to be.

It's hard to deal with each kid and every situation as though it's a first. But once you say, "I've met his type before," or "That's typical of adolescents," you're dangerously close to falling back on the script. If you can keep from generalizing—from robbing kids of their uniqueness—it's an easy ride. Without even trying, you meet kids as individuals; you establish dynamic relationships; you work with them, instead of banging at doors and bemoaning the lack of communication between generations.

Repeat: There is nothing easier than being yourself. When I'm mad, I yell. When something's funny, I laugh. And I saw no reason why the kids shouldn't have as much fun as I did. I tried to see to it that they succeeded. Success is great fun.

Because I'm not a role player, the kids had a hard time. It's easy to work for a teacher type. It's hard when you're dealing with a real person. Real people are inconsistent. My kids responded well to familiar structure. They really wanted Monday to be vocabulary day and Tuesday to be composition. I can't work that way. So they were nervous wrecks, which I loved—it made for a nice, noisy classroom.

When we were discussing Death of a Salesman, I asked the class to report on several of the characters in terms of whether or not they were victims of circumstance. After the class had their say, I had mine. Sedrick Powell waited for me to finish carrying on about the play and related issues, like whether slum people are trapped by the ghetto. Then he said, "Why can't you ever give us both sides of a story?" and I had to launch into a defensive harangue about hypocrisy and middle-of-the-roaders.

But somehow, my inconsistencies worked for me. I could scream, "That's the dumbest thing I ever heard!" and the kids knew I meant, "You're too smart to make a crack like that." I got away with murder.

When a situation arose that I just couldn't handle, I told the kids. There would have been no point in pretending—they could spot a phony a mile away. I found there was almost nothing they couldn't take care of, be it a kid having an epileptic seizure, or a crowd of boys

I didn't know, who'd drop in to disrupt things, or a discussion that would turn to pandemonium.

Calvin Rush was one of the North Corner gang. They're the kids who kill the most people, fight the most cops, and terrorize a rather large section of the city. Calvin was a tough kid, and his class was a particularly difficult one. So it was only natural that I turned to him the first week of school to get the class I didn't yet know to stay in their seats and off one another's throats. I was timid about asking favors of him; he never spoke or smiled; he just sat in the back of the room and looked hostile. But I needed help, and though there are hazards involved in committing yourself to bully power, I decided they were worth the risk. I didn't realize until weeks later that I had made my first ally of the year in Calvin. Like many of the boys, he became quite protective of me, and did everything possible to spare me any uncomfortable moments. Had I pretended to be in command of the situation, never turning to anyone for help, I'd probably still be fighting to establish my position as head of the class, or authoritarian, or earth mother, or something. But my aide took his job very seriously. I could concentrate on teaching, because Calvin had the behavioral situation well in control.

As a teacher type, I would have had little hope of making the kids produce. They didn't care about grades or college recommendations, so there was nothing to threaten them with. When they worked, it was because they wanted to. They seemed to know that my homework wasn't busy work. It was stuff that just couldn't be done in a fifty-minute class period. So they did it. Because it made sense.

When I first started to teach, every funny or sad or poignant thing that happened at school became talk and thought material for weeks. I wrote down every great remark the kids made, and ran home to babble about latest events.

Time, however, wore away the newness of it all. I got annoyed at myself when a visitor in my class laughed hysterically at something a kid said, and I hadn't been alert enough to know what it was. I was jaded.

Anyway, I guess that's why I wasn't as horrified as the public seemed to be when word leaked through school and the newspapers that one of our boys had been shot through the head by a gang. I don't understand gang warfare, but I know it's a fact of life. The kids play war just as fervently as grownups do. They have to protect their territory and make it safe to walk the streets; they have to assert their power; they have to vent their hatreds. The life of a boy matters little when such issues are at stake. So Danny Simms was dead.

The kids who were there when it happened said I was right outside in my car at a stop light. It was a nice day, and I remember seeing a group of kids outside the corner drugstore. The light turned green and I headed home, not knowing that a car coming in the opposite direction carried three boys, a girl, and a gun. They'd run into the drugstore, shot Danny, and fled.

I got the story the next day. Four of the North Corner boys were in my fifth-period class, and the two who were in school filled me in on the details. The absentees had been picked up by the police for questioning.

"Brint and Crow? But they're so nice—did they do it?" The kids said they didn't, so I felt better. I couldn't wait till they got back to school.

At lunch with the teachers, I learned the real irony of the situation. Danny's mother, one of the very few active mothers in the neighborhood, had met with the superintendent of schools the day before the murder. She had gone to protest the overcrowding at school and to tell the school board that she was afraid for her son—that the school was not a safe place for him.

The apathy of ghetto people is an awful problem. And when a few parents make the effort to deal with a frighteningly large institution—when they finally get mad enough to do something about the rotten state of their lives—they deserve to be heard. They don't need a dead son to point up the futility of their fight.

Mrs. Simms—of all people. It was a damn lousy deal. Brint was back at school in a few days. He said they were holding Crow and three other kids. I asked him if one of them was guilty, and he said yes, but it wasn't Crow. I let it drop.

It was several weeks before Crow came back. I saw him in the hall one morning and gave him a big hello. We talked about jail for a while. He said it wasn't bad, but the cops roughed him up a lot. And that he was just out on bail—there was a trial in a couple of months. I asked him about the three others who'd been held.

"Yeah, they're out too," he said.

"Did one of them do it?"

"Yeah."

I really wanted to be in on it all. I begged him to tell me who shot Danny.

"Aw, come on, Miss Deck, you don't really spec me to tell you that, do you?"

"Of course not," I said—and meant it. But I was a little put off anyway. He smiled, and we said good-by. Crow stopped coming to school several weeks later, and I never saw him again.

But one Friday, there was a big story in the paper, headlined "Four Youths Freed of Murder Charge." It went on to describe an awkward moment at the end of the trial when the dead boy's mother, on hearing the verdict, jumped up and screamed, "They're murderers—they killed my son!" The paper suggested what a nuisance it is that some people just can't behave in court.

The article also mentioned Speed Green, one of the witnesses. Speed was in my eleventh-grade class. And he'd never even told me he was in on it! Again, I felt left out. Apparently, he'd signed a statement naming the kid who shot Danny, but on the stand, said he had been forced by police to sign it, and he didn't remember what happened.

I guess the North Corner boys had scared him to death. And it's understandable. You're in court for just a few minutes—but you have to face the street every day. The judge could only be mad at him for changing his story. If he'd talked, the kids would have killed him. He did the only thing he could. I mean, you've got to take care of yourself. No one else will.

The simple ability to accept people and situations at face value is new to me. I've always had to explain and categorize behavior to feel comfortable about it. But that's the kind of stuff that makes you old.

You begin to generalize.

James Smith, for example, spent the first week of school with his roster card upside down. The only thing that didn't please him was the fact that the blocks of the card that showed his lunch period came first thing in the morning. He said he wasn't hungry then.

I suggested that he turn his roster around, thereby moving lunch from the top of the card to the bottom—one-thirty seemed a more appropriate time. I was timid about it—in situations like that I always wonder if it's me and not the kid.

James Smith just stared. The weight of his fat lower lip tugged his jaw open.

Look, you've got seven periods, yes? If you turn them around, one is where seven was, and two where six was, and three where five was, yes? So if it says you go to room 325 fifth period and you turn the card around, you go there *third* period, yes? And howcum you can read upside down anyway?

We righted the card, and I waited for light to dawn on that thin, placid face. His too-round eyes moved from the roster to me. "That's not my roster," said James Smith.

"But that's your *name*—the other way you couldn't read your *name!*" I was getting panicky.

"Oh yes I could."

I told him to do as I said, and strode off like I was a big-deal teacher with somewhere to go.

The next day, James Smith was sitting in my fifth-period class. I was sure the teacher who used that room third period would miss him. But from then on, everything was fine. Really.

Then one day, James Smith came up to my desk after class. He just stood there, until everyone else had left. Then, "Miss, can I ask you a big favor?"

"Why, of course, James," said I.

"Will you call me Arnold?"

Why not? Everyone else in the world calls him James. But when I walk down the hall and yell, "Hey, Arnold," he glows. So, why not?

I learned the same sort of lesson when I asked Alan Cohen how black people got to be Jewish.

"You join a synagogue," he said.

It was that simple.

A new September. On the first day, all the old kids stopped in to say hi. I loved seeing them, and their appearance in my class made me look pretty good to the new kids who were sizing me up. None of the summer's important changes struck me that day. I was too busy recognizing familiar faces. I nearly died when I saw Felice.

Felice Obiece had been the fattest female in the world. I used to call her Obiece Felice. She worked hard for her A.

Somewhere between our last class in June and the beginning of the fall term, she lost a ton. Her face was still round and spongy, but the rest of her looked great. When I passed her in a crowded corridor, I didn't recognize her until she'd repeated my name three times.

"Felice! Look at you!" I was delighted, so I screamed. She shushed me and fled down the hall, leaving me to wipe off the spray of skinny saliva. Under her black skin she must have been blushing like mad. I saw her several times after that. Her eyes smiled at me, and her finger slapped itself across full, pursed lips. I didn't dare open my mouth. I guess she was passing for someone else.

Several of the old kids appeared on my roll sheet, and I promised I'd have them transferred out—everyone's entitled to a clean slate. Besides, they knew me far too well, and that's scary.

Frankie Horn kept in close touch, even though he had someone else for English.

He stopped in to chat at least once a week, and we really got to know each other. His father died in the fall, and his mother was in the hospital, so Frankie was job hunting. He had to take care of the five younger kids at home. He was terribly depressed, and I worried about him. Then a great thing happened. I stopped at a swanky little flower shop one day to get some fall colors, and the owner, whom I'd known casually for a couple years, struck up a conversation about school.

I told him a little about it, and he carried on about what a marvelous job I was doing and how he'd always wanted to do something for these poor kids.

"All right," I said. "Hire Frankie Horn." And he did!

It took hours before I found Frankie's phone number (I couldn't possibly have waited till the next day), and I explained everything to him—the hours, the pay—it was an awfully good job. He didn't scream and yell like I did, but I could tell he was excited.

I drove him to work every day, since it was on my way home, and delighted in everything he reported. He was really learning. He hadn't run into many flowers before, he said, so it was hard at first, but in a week he'd learned most of the flowers they stocked. He was still confusing roses and carnations, but he thought he'd have it before long. I was furious when I found out he wasn't being paid the two dollars an hour I'd been promised. I guess even the best-intentioned people panic when you hit them in the wallet. Frankie made me promise not to go to the boss. He was afraid I'd make a scene and jeopardize his job. I agreed, but grudgingly.

The week before Christmas he announced that he'd saved enough money to buy his mother a hundred-dollar watch. Big shot. I told him I thought he was a jerk, and you don't buy watches till you can feed your family. He laughed a little and said it all depends what's important to you. His mother had always wanted a watch. All her life.

I got some Christmas cards from Frankie's old classmates, which was nice, though most of them were pretty Jesusy.

And Bernice's new English teacher told me that when she'd asked her class to write the nicest thing that ever happened to them in school, Bernice answered, "Writing haiku for Mrs. Decker."

I saw Frankie only twice after Christmas. Then he disappeared. Weeks later I stopped in to see his counselor and asked if she knew anything. She said Frankie's mother had moved to New Jersey, so of course, he'd gone too. Just like that.

"Did you expect him to kiss you good-by?" she joked.

I said I didn't know.

I'd lost Frankie. I'd also lost all claim to a classroom.

"You are," announced Adolf Farber, "a floater," as though he'd just discovered I was a junkie.

"A who?"

I found out quickly. A floater is like a human Mack truck. You have all the books, papers, and tools of a real teacher, but no classroom to call your own. A minor rostering problem. So you take it with you. Plus your coat, umbrella, paper clips, and the last copy of *Time* you'll read before you *absolutely* cancel your subscription.

I felt like a kid again, racing to each class, hoping that this time I'd make it without falling or dropping something or sweating. Being a floater keeps you where the action is—in the hallway. The only time I really had to get comfortable was in my double period—a phenomenon of public school more akin to an endurance test.

The double period of English was set up for very slow tenth-graders who aren't quite slow enough for a reading program. Most teachers hate it—it's hard to fill an hour and a half, especially when the concentration span of your kids is ten minutes. Besides, they'd rather teach brighter students.

My advantage over such teachers was that my concentration span is as short as the kids', and my conception of teaching has little to do with how quick the students are. I loved the chance to work with one kid at a time and develop the intimacy that accompanies that kind of tutoring. So I spent half the time with the class as a whole, and half the time working with individual students, while the class did independent work. Since there were thirty kids in the class, I could hit maybe five or six a day, thereby seeing everyone once a week. It was a nice way to spend an hour. And by the time class was dismissed, I could face another charge down the hall.

I figured this would be a good year to lose weight. Changing classes was great, frantic exercise, and I'd decided to climb stairs instead of suffering the dumb conversation in the faculty elevator. It was going to be a thin semester.

The kids seemed older this year. It may have been the bushes. Only a few of the boys still wore processed hair. The others had swung with the tide of the summer. It was exciting to see the indications of change.

The summer had done it. It made Martin Luther King an Uncle Tom. It made an in-group of the black nationalists.

Not everyone had become the active thinker his hair and dress indicated, though. When I saw Dennis Hower walking around in beads, I realized that for many it was just the fashion. Dennis had never had a thought in his head. I hoped that if he let all the woolly hair out on the outside, his brain might be less entangled and start to work. Fat chance.

For every two Dennis Howers, though, there was a kid who had begun to act and question and challenge society. I searched my classes for them. And who did I find?

For the second year in a row, I had Byron Thurmond. And I knew by the end of the first quarter of the year that for the second year in a row, I'd flunk him. Like most kids', Byron's F's had nothing to do with his brain. It was his extracurricular activities that cut me out of his schedule, and thereby cut his average to nothing. Last year, he was busy with fatherly duties. He was forever taking his two sons to the zoo or the park and parading them in and out of school (though never during class time). The year was spent in celebration of Byron Thurmond's virility.

This year it was Black Unity. The father bit somehow wore off over the summer. And besides, he couldn't afford to let his militant friends know that the mother of his children was an Italian girl from South Philly. Fraternizing with whites just doesn't make it these days.

Though I didn't see him very often, I enjoyed our visits tremendously. I felt in no way obliged to discipline him or talk teacher. He was nearly twenty, and the draft board would grab him as soon as his grades were low enough to qualify him.

He was a first-class con artist, and I'd spent a good deal of time listening to his new plans for seriousing up. Sometimes he would stick to them for as long as twenty minutes.

Lawrence Lucas and Byron were in the same class. They made quite a team. It wasn't long ago that Lawrence explained all the factions of the black organizations to me and added that he hadn't joined any because he knew too much about them—just as he was beginning to get interested in a group, he'd always find out something he didn't agree with. I felt very proud to know him. He was remarkably well informed, and I was as impressed with his manner as I was with his appraisal of the world around him.

But that was the old Lawrence. In three brief months, he became an organization man. He was still a charmer, but he didn't engage me in dialogue any more. He ran around in his African clothes and led marches, and when he talked, talked at me, not to me. When the black nationalists won Lawrence Lucas, they got a good thing.

One day, Byron made one of his rare appearances in class. There was a motive, of course. He had this Malcolm X record I should please play. Since I agreed, some of the black-power kids cut their own classes and came to listen. Lawrence brought a great-looking boy he introduced as Lamonte MacArthur. He was as tall and handsome as Lawrence, and he impressed me with a certain sophistication I lack—a sureness and ease about himself and those around him. I hoped I was looking old in my green suit. I had the feeling that if the kids knew I was only four years older than they, the thin air of authority I had would disappear.

I turned on the record player and watched the class watch me as Malcolm X yelled obscenities at whites.

Byron looked slightly apologetic, as though he was afraid I'd take the record too personally and think he'd brought it with the intention of hurting my feelings. Every time Malcolm said something vicious, Byron winced a little.

For twenty minutes all forty of us listened. Lawrence alone seemed not to hear. He kept staring at his guest in such a way that I got the feeling that Lamonte MacArthur sat somewhat higher than Lawrence in the power structure, and that Lawrence was doing his best to impress him. I suddenly saw Lawrence differently. He was, all of a sudden, just a good-looking kid. It was disappointing.

Malcolm X ended his tirade, and I exploded with a few points I had jotted down while listening. The record had made me mad. I am convinced that I'm not a blue-eyed, blond-haired pilgrim, as Malcolm painted me, and that my kids are not slaves in shackles. They're kids—city kids, living under the stigma of their color and their poverty. And I'm a dark-haired Russian, here only because my great-grandfather smuggled himself over on a stolen passport. I said exactly that, and the debate was on. The room was noisy, because kids make a lot of noise when they think. It was hard to hear individual comments and answer them.

So when Lamonte MacArthur started laughing it up with the girl next to him, I got annoyed. Guest or no, he wasn't going to turn my discussion into confused racket.

I never even thought about Lawrence Lucas, who wanted so much for Lamonte to enjoy his visit. I just barked, "Look, Lamonte, if you're going to come to my class, you're going to pay attention!"

The sharpness in my voice silenced the class. Lawrence looked at me, and Lawrence looked at Lamonte. Then he grinned and cocked his head to a jaunty angle.

"Hey, Lamonte," he said, "see how my teach remembers your name?"

Thus, early in the year, I became O.K., for a white chick, with the group I was to see little, hear about often, and hate, as they forced me to wrestle with new ideas. Like most people, I resist change, and had to be forced to acknowledge it.

I got wind of it one autumn Wednesday—just that there was going to be a walkout at noon tomorrow. And that Will Palmer was going to speak. I said his name was *Walt* Palmer, and what was he going to speak about that was worth walking out for. No one seemed to know. Eddie Albers said he was walking out. I asked why. "Because if a black man tells me to walk out, I'm gonna walk out." I suggested that if a black man asked him to jump off a cliff, he'd jump off a cliff. He got furious. It was a bad way for me to lose.

The kids were different this year. Last year, when my sophomores had a debate on Black Power, I couldn't get anyone to be on the militant side. The riots embarrassed them; they were too afraid or too indoctrinated by traditional ideology or too rational to yield to extremes.

they riots for little things like if a white man call a person black they start up a riot. when all the person half to do is say what he half to say back to the white man.

I would like to be reborn in California I'd prefer Los Angeles. Change my race to white because I admire them Don't get me wrong I'm proud to be a negro. Its just that we don't know how to act or respect our fellow man.

The riots as I see them are conducted by madmen all they do is make more trouble for themself.

In general I think the negro's position in America is, FAiR Could Be Better if They Know how to Ack.

This year, I was told to forget the word "Negro." They were the blacks. Lots of the kids were just hostile. Only a few knew anything about legislation or the leaders of their movements. The vast majority knew only that unity among blacks was suddenly vital. And they were unified in hate.

I didn't know much about the movements at that time, but I told the kids what I knew and asked lots of questions. They didn't have much to offer. They hated whitey, there was going to be a black revolution, and walking out of school was a neat thing to do.

I hear the student leaders go to freedom classes at night and on weekends. They know what's going on. At least, they know half of what's going on. The masses are just the pawns. They can always be counted on to follow.

I'd been aware of the new atmosphere in school, but I'd never really been concerned. I was banking on this, like all extremes, phasing itself out.

I talked to two classes Wednesday afternoon, and three the next morning, with varying results. It's funny how a class develops group personality. Some were honest and vocal. My second period, a class of forty-six, was silent. They just glared at me. Maybe there were some who were intimidated by the size of the class, and unwilling to let it be known that they were not haters. I found out later that a lot of kids had been threatened. They were told they'd be hurt if they didn't participate in the walkout. But I didn't know that then. I felt it was my skin that had made them silent. Everything I said seemed stilted and wrong. My voice sounded horrible to me. For a whole hour, they just sat and stared while I tried to fill the space between us.

By ten o'clock Thursday morning there were four cops at every door. There were plain-clothes men in the lunchroom. I went to the vice principal and suggested that he disconnect the fire bell to avoid any unscheduled exodus from the building. He told me not to worry my pretty head.

At ten of twelve there was a fire alarm. I told my sophomores to sit still and open your books to page twenty. I waited for the vice principal to come and apologize, but he never showed.

We worked for a few minutes. But it was stupid to pretend everything was fine, because everything was awful and we all knew it. At five of twelve I said, "There are many causes in this world worth dying for. I know I'd be willing to pay a price for something I believed in. At twelve o'clock some of you are planning to walk out of here. I'm certainly not dumb enough to stand in the doorway and let you walk over me. But before anyone leaves, I'd like a reason—I'd like to know why you're going."

They snorted a little to each other, and a few kids put on their coats. I waited, and it felt very like a showdown in a bad western. After an awkward minute, I began to realize that no one had anything to say. Whether my one-sided discussions had had any effect or whether they were just too inarticulate to explain themselves, or whether they were scared, I don't know. But no one moved. I handed out some magazines and told them to read.

It was hard to make sense of the sounds we heard during the next half-hour. The bell rang, signaling the end of fifth period. Since this was my double-period tenth grade, my kids could only listen to the excitement in the halls. They were trapped with me for another fifty minutes. During the change of classes, the fire alarm sounded again, urging everyone to take advantage of the chance to leave the building. The noise in the hall grew louder.

Police cars pulled up outside the windows. The not knowing was frightening, but I had begun to sense that the kids and I were on the same side, and that was a nice feeling. We talked a little about the rally in the schoolyard, and what the school might do to people who participated. I think I was as much a comfort to the kids as they were to me.

Gwendolyn Williams said she smelled smoke. "Ah ha!" I said. "You don't think I'm gonna fall for that one, do you? You can't put me on." I was smug.

"No, really—there's smoke!" They were awfully good at this routine. I just grinned at them. But when they offered to stay in their seats while I went to check on it, I agreed—they were so insistent. I tried to look condescending, opened the door, and walked into a cloud. The kids were too scared to be delighted. I wasn't scared at all. I felt like an ass.

Leaving them on oath to stay in class, I ran to another room to find help. It never occurred to me that there might be no help—that I had been isolated from anything that might have happened. John Minsky, a science teacher, was sitting at his desk, playing with a test tube. There were some students wandering around the room. I told him to find the fire and let us know if evacuation was in order. Then I went back to class. I always hated teachers who said, "Oh, it's nothing," and never told us what "it" was. So I said there was a lot of smoke. There were no questions. I heard later on the radio that our smoke had been one of three fires.

At one o'clock, I went to my next class. In the five minutes between classes, I got a look outside. Red cars were bumper to bumper around the school. There were reporters with cameras and police and hundreds of kids marching around the school behind a great-looking guy wearing a beard and African garb. It must have been Palmer. He was a born leader. There was something strong and magnetic about him. I wished I'd been outside to hear him.

There were twenty-five kids in class when I arrived. I couldn't believe it. They were all in their seats, and no one said a word. I asked them what they were doing there—it seemed ridiculous not to take advantage of the chaos and cut class, if only to go to the lunchroom. They said there was a riot in the lunchroom. People were throwing plates. A teacher had been beaten up.

I thought we'd get through the period better if we did something, so I began the lesson. Within five minutes I couldn't hear myself talk. Mobs of people came surging up the stairs, shrieking, knocking over each other, hurtling down the halls.

I found out later that the board of education, in a statement typical of Establishment idiocy, had ordered that "any student who leaves the building must be given an opportunity to return." The doors had been unlocked, and the crowd from the street returned to join forces with the crowd in the cafeteria. The mob numbered well over two thousand now, and its size gave it the nerve to unleash its hostility. It was my first experience with mob rule. It was a frantic, explosive, unreasoned thing.

While the riot raged, a hundred cops stood outside twirling their night sticks and sucking their thumbs. The press, also safely out in the street, reported that the rally was orderly, though there was some shouting and shoving, and that the students returned to their classes at one-fifteen P.M.

My class seemed as frightened as I was. It was the only time in my life when I felt that regardless of what happened, there was nothing I could do to protect myself or help the kids. The class suggested that I move away from the door so I couldn't be seen from the hall. I wished I was colored.

The noise outside the room was deafening. Since there was no point in trying to talk, we just sat there. Every few minutes, the door would fly open and people would run in yelling, "Let's go—let's kill those honkies!" or "Some girl got trampled to death!" or "Whatsa matter, you chicken?" No one moved. It was one of those unexplainable miracles. Finally the kids said, "It's all right if you lock the door." I never would have suggested it myself. I wanted to say thank you, but it seemed corny, so I went to the door; the lock didn't work.

It was a long time before the bell rang. Somehow, everyone knew school had been dismissed. Two boys offered to walk me to my car. Since it was warm for October, I drove with the windows open.

That day was a violent introduction to a new era for me. Last year, I don't think it ever occurred to me that my kids were different from any others. After the first few days of school, I never noticed color. Since there weren't any white students in the school, racial tensions never cropped up. I discussed civil rights as I would have in any school. The kids, for the most part, were pretty unconcerned with such topics. The problems of getting through each day left no time for bigger issues. Money, gangs, food, and family are immediate things. And they can keep you too busy to worry about Detroit or some other remote place. So I forgot they were colored. They were just kids—with big problems and neat ideas.

just about all over me everything is like I want it. everything except my hands they seem as though they don't belong to me.

When I was about nine year old my mother what getting very sick until she had to go ~~to the or~~ to the   and then a man came to to my grandmother house and he said that my mother had die last ~~our~~ night   I can't never forget that day as long as I ~~live~~ live

I would like to be a boy. The reason I say this is, because they don't have to go though all the changes we do, like having children, and rising them and menstruction perio. They can go any where they want to any time they want to and don't have to worry about being rape or someone trying to kidnap them. They have a good advantage

YOUR FAMILY LEFT
LEAVING NOT A thing FOR YOU
BECAUSE tHEY WERE POOR

I would like to be somebody that never be push around because everybody are way laughing at me and they make me fill bad that I think that I think that I don't have have any friend in the world. The only reason I telling you because if I had told somebody els they would just had laugh at me and call me cazy

The thing in my life that has made me most unhappy when my mother die. She was the only parent I had in the world.

You don't have it to have cool money to be rich

They were just kids.

I got a letter from Regina Wilson the day after the riot. It was her way of reacting. None of us had really begun to think yet.

Yesterday about 12:00 I was very upset about how most of the boys and girls of North High School were acting. They were runing up and down the halls making so much nose that you could not here yourself talk, even at one time they knocked a teacher down they were throughing dishing around the lunch room braching fire alome they also beat some girl up because she said that she was not going to walk out. To me none of this make any seens because what did we gather not a thing and to me it don't make any different because the way I stongly fell is that God terate us all equal.

It was like the day after Christmas—very empty, very anticlimactic. Everyone felt lousy, and because no one would talk, there was a tension that was unendurable. Everyone in town was discussing it—we even made the New York Times—but in school no one said a word. At an emergency faculty meeting, it was agreed, in true Establishment style, that "something has to be done." The administration had met with the black-power leaders to discuss their grievances and learned a few things: The school is overcrowded—it was built for 1,700, and we have 4,300 students—the food in the lunchroom is terrible; the kids don't want to salute the flag. Everyone agreed that committees should be formed to remedy these situations—but we should be careful not to let the kids know that their behavior triggered our action—that might encourage them. Say—wouldn't it be nice to have a faculty-student committee to discuss these problems? And for God's sake put telephones in the classrooms so teachers can call for help if they need it. And on and on.

But I have the feeling that we're just too late. The issues being negotiated are only symptomatic, and not at all the core of the problem. The kids really don't care whether we form a committee or not. They waited for that kind of communication for a long time, and now they have taken action alone. Their movements are far more organized and unified than any group could be in a system choking on red tape. They have proved their strength. They have no need of us.

Our principal has meetings with self-appointed leaders of the black nationalists. I'm not sure why. Maybe he is afraid to ignore them. Maybe they really are officials of a black nation I won't admit exists.

People who are more informed than I on the activities around the school make remarks about all the people who ignored Hitler in his early days. I tell them not to be stupid—that this isn't the same at all.

Yet I'm convinced that the worst is still ahead of us. I think the black world—the ghetto world—has given up on us.

it could improve. It all up to togetherness).

*The Negroes will never get no where
This is Charlies world and we are here just to
keep it going.*

It took a long time for me to be convinced there'd been a basic change in the kids over the summer. It was easy to write off the things said during the riot—anyone can get sucked in by that kind of fervor. It was the little things that drove the point home—the new batch of haikus; open-ended composition topics; classroom happenings.

It was one of those discussions about social inequities. Everyone was yelling like mad, trying to make his point, when Earl Abner slammed his books on the desk. We all shut up.

"Look at television!" he screamed. "Like commercials—you never see Negroes in commercials." The cords in his neck stood out. "You know that Listerine commercial? You know, you never see Negroes in Listerine commercials, and I know for a fact—" he shook his fist—"I know for a fact that some Negroes have bad breath!"

In written assignments, I never asked for comment on racial issues. I'd just say, "Write about a sadness," or "Use what you've learned about poetry to compose a poem about something outside your private world." Few kids would miss the chance to make a point. The change was obvious: Their blackness had become the issue.

*A mass of hands reaching for me
Grabbing at me—Trying to snuff out my life
Squeezing, choking*

*Why am I to be destroyed?
Why are the hands white?*

I'm a black man
my family is black people
so I am hated

What rights Do we have
We have the right to protest
Where will it get us

I Love my Country
I believe in religion
I have lost my pride

Mother and Father
Without you I would not be
With you I learned hate

All is gay and bright,
Things seem privileged and free
Negro has to fight

Black is a good thing //
I know It is a good, thing
Why do I feel bad /

Think life is all pleasure?
Now look at me, my child, look
Is it or is it not

There's a whole world I don't know anything about. It's embarrassing—because I'm living in it. And it's a blow to my ego to learn that
I've been blithering along with blinders on. Ted Johnson approached
me one day with a plan to get faculty members together in the
evening to discuss racial issues and hack out differences. I shut him
up real fast with some remark about our faculty being a pretty bright
bunch with rather unusual *esprit de corps.* "Where the hell have you
been?" he asked. I didn't know.

So, to find out, I began to hang around the faculty room and ask
questions. It was a whole new thing. My life at school had been in
the classroom; my reactions to racial issues had been on a one-to-one
basis. I guess I've just heard so many generalizations and pat remarks
in the past few years, I've closed myself off to anything that begins
with, "the white power structure," or "the blacks of this country."
Grownups say things like that. So I turned them off. I could hate
Morris Feldman for his revolting behavior with Elvira that day in the
crowded hall. But I never thought of him as a representative of a
white society. I may have been wrong.

Anyway, I started to nose around the grownups. I listened to a black lady and a white lady talk race. The white lady was a screaming liberal, who'd done all sorts of great things for the colored girl who cleaned her house. She couldn't understand the girl's nasty attitude. "How old is your girl?" asked the black lady. "Oh, fortyish." The black lady smiled a little and said quietly, "How old must she be before she'll be a woman?"

Carol Ramp talked about the Negro high school she'd attended as a kid. She was in the choir. And whenever they went to sing at a white school, they were told to "show them how nice you can act."

"I spent my life showing them," she says. "And when I'd showed them all by graduating from college, I moved to Baltimore and got a good job, and found out when I went to a department store that they were very happy to sell me a girdle. Just as long as I didn't want to try it on."

I sure have been dumb. I always got upset when a Negro made categorical statements to me about whites. If I could react to people as individuals, why couldn't they? I'm beginning to see, now.

Dwaine Bulford told me he didn't think of me as a white.

"I came into your room the first day of school and started actin' crazy, and you just laughed," he said. "You could walk down the hall in a riot, and no one would hurt you cause we know how you are."

Until now, I'd just assumed that. It's a damn shame I have to feel proud of it.

I guess the nicest part about being white is that I could remain so naïve for so long. I've got it made. I don't have to fight with myself to see people as individuals. I don't have a past full of indignities that I remember every time I meet another one of "them." I don't have to work at forgetting anything.

Eli Butler stood up at a faculty meeting one day to discuss the problems of black people in the city.

"Just remember," he said to us, "that I can go to a gas station two blocks from here and they'll call me boy."

That's the way it is.

Ted Johnson's meeting was held on a rainy Tuesday night, at one of the other teacher's homes. I'm not a meeting-attender, and I knew

full well that most dialogues turn into diatribes, but I went anyway. There had been so many questions raised on racial and educational issues, and I was so in need of a perspective I felt I lacked, that I was sure I'd learn something from an integrated group of involved people. What I learned: Mrs. Howard, who entertained us, has plastic covers on her furniture; Mrs. Nugent looks lousy in slacks; the fat old ladies I'd been putting down showed up in force; the black teachers didn't come, except for six; Sandra Knight's a bigot. I also learned that I have more common sense than I gave myself credit for. That was the nicest part of the evening.

Everyone had come to make a speech. Miraculously, we were oracles. No one seemed able to respond to anyone else. People insisted on prefacing statements with phrases like "all black kids" and "no white teacher." I was the only person who asked a question. It went unanswered. But the coffee cake was pretty good.

Essentially, I wanted to know whether I'd underplayed the role of color—whether there is a barrier between blacks and whites that no one ever transcends. There was no consensus. The cry of the angry black teachers was of course there's a barrier, because you can't pretend to be black. One white liberal was fist-pounding that no white could ever have soul—and you can't reach These Kids without soul.

I don't know. There are elements in every argument that make sense. I'll buy reaching kids—but does it take a black soul to do it? I'll also buy color as an influence in the classroom. It's easier to respond to someone you can identify with, and there's no more obvious badge than color.

But in lieu of a great, black teacher, I will not believe that some hostile, pretentious dodo will be more effective than I am just because she's black.

By the end of the evening, I was furious at everything that had not been communicated. For the most part, though, the others who attended felt pretty good. Teachers just love to talk.

The next day I greeted my class with, "Guess what I learned last night." And since they couldn't, "That a black teacher works with you better than a white teacher—and you can understand each other more because the black-white thing is gone."

A couple of kids nodded. A few shrugged their shoulders. Lots of them smiled. Otis said, "Hey, lady, you're too smart to say something like that."

We talked about the faculty. There was a good deal of agreement. "They got a longer temper here."

"The older people are more prejudiced about whites. They've had it harder."

What emerged was the balance I've come to count on. The kids had an unshakable perspective that they lost only in moments when the mob took over. I needed them and their clear view of things more than I ever imagined. I felt better talking with them. But I felt I ought to end the discussion and begin to teach. It's not fair for me to do all the learning.

Even when I work at it, I'm still a disappointment to myself. There's so much the kids should learn, and I used to get frantic trying to get it all in and make it stick. Sometimes I was sure I was the lousiest teacher in the world. I had just read another news article about a guy in New York who was superimaginative, and superdedicated, and who made his teaching a twenty-four-hour-a-day job. Which made me look bad. I raced the kids to the door on Friday afternoons—and other days, too. My lessons bored me stiff half the time. All winter, I prayed for a school-closing blizzard. The scariest part of my rotten attitude was that I was losing my sense of humor. On one awful Tuesday, I didn't laugh once.

I yelled at King Copeley for doing exactly the opposite of what I'd directed, and he reminded me that he was a human being and I should talk to him like one. He was right, of course, and I told him so. But I just got so tired of the same hassles day after day. I have so little patience, and it wears so thin!

Eliot was wrong. It's January that's the cruelest month. No vacations in sight, dark mornings, and cold days. It was an endless month. One quarter of the school was absent every day, and another quarter was late. It took many of the kids more than an hour of buses and trolleys to get to school, and you really couldn't blame them for not wanting to stand on a dismal corner at 7 A.M. Especially to make my eight o'clock class. I found it nearly impossible to put on a great show at that hour. And since I was dull and irritable, the kids were awful. So I got really irritable. So they got worse.

Although I would have liked to believe they were a hopeless bunch, I couldn't. Their classroom attitude was always a reflection of my mood. They would take my bitching gracefully once in a while, but not as a steady diet.

After an especially deadly week, I resolved to make a drastic change in my classes. The kids couldn't stand me, and I couldn't stand myself. I spoke to a couple of the more imaginative teachers, and milked them for some radical, creative ideas. The hardest part of the reformation was working up enough initiative to begin again—to build some new units, and introduce them with enthusiasm. But I guess we usually manage to do what's necessary, and this was vital.

I never really understood what a unit was. Those Who Know tell you it's a group of varied but related activities centered on a theme. You want kids to read, write, talk, think, take tests, and be creative. So instead of doing something creative on Monday, then reading a story on Tuesday, and writing an essay the next day, you pick a concept—like love. You find everything you can that relates to love, or lack of love: books, poems, pictures, music, essay topics, vocabulary words. Then you allow this wealth of material to unfold before them like a flower, each petal growing from one stem and overlapping with others. Sounds great. The only hitch is that it's impossible. Compositions don't emerge from kids who can't write. Books don't get read when you've got forty kids and thirty books and ten excuses a day. And you can't slip in a stimulating debate when no one knows how to use library books for research, or make notes for a speech.

If you're going to do anything right, it takes drilling from the ground up. You're too busy teaching particulars to worry about the flower of a unit.

I attempted something simple. All I wanted was a change of pace that would be both profitable and fun. So I organized a week of role-playing, group discussion, and personality study with two classes. In my seventh-period class, it was a great success. The class ran itself; the kids discovered each other; we were a happy group. In my slow class of forty-two eleventh-graders, it flopped. They said they'd rather learn something.

It was hard to get my tenth-grade class out of their rut. They were the group some people call "retarded educable." It's an awful label. They were great kids—they just couldn't read. I gave them copies of West Side Story, and after we'd plowed through it, I suggested we dramatize it.

For the next two weeks, I was a very unimportant member of the class. The kids organized their forces, cast parts, and wrote their own script. I began to be impressed, not just by the intensity of their effort, but by the quality of their acting. They were naturals. They rehearsed endlessly, and had little patience with those who wouldn't cooperate. The leaders of the group ran the class like a military unit. I didn't want the project to die in the classroom, so I arranged to have them make a television tape which could be shown on closed-circuit TV in school. (We have all sorts of equipment for that sort of thing, since we're a slum school. No books, but a TV in every room.)

The kids were thrilled. They worked like fiends to perfect their art. They humiliated anyone who forgot his lines, and censored weak parts of the script with, "Hey, man, no one says that jive stuff—say it this way." Attendance jumped to 90 per cent.

A couple of days before we were to tape, I brought up the subject of props. We needed a gun. I explained that I'm terrified of guns—even unloaded ones, so I'd like a cap gun. Could anyone produce one? No. All right, who's got a real one? Every hand in the class went up. I picked someone I trusted a lot, and asked him if he'd promise to bring blanks instead of bullets. He swore he would. It was settled.

The next day the gun was on my desk. I suggested that I be the one to carry it around so the owner wouldn't get caught with it in school. He agreed, and I stashed it in my purse. All day, I walked around with it. All day, I felt like a big shot.

The taping session was exciting. Everything went beautifully—until my offstage part: I couldn't make the gun shoot! While the actors froze, waiting for the blast, I tried like mad to make it work, with no luck. Finally someone said, "Squeeze it, Miss Deck—slowly!" I squoze—and was so frantic by then, I forgot to aim at the floor. When the gun finally exploded, it was pointed directly at the star of the play. And it was a blank. I sure am lucky.

When the tape was finished, everyone crowded around the TV. The kids got to watch themselves, and I got to watch them watching. It was a great treat. They squeezed each other's hands, and giggled, and grinned like crazy. It wasn't at all like January.

The returns are more than worth the effort. That's why it surprises me that there are so many lousy teachers running around. It takes so little effort to plan projects that will excite kids. Of course, the person thing plays a part, too. Some people just can't be human with students. You see them talk to kids in the hallway, and you wonder how they've managed to survive for so long.

You'd think people would learn. There are certain techniques that just don't work with kids. Our kids, because they had so much to be defensive about, were awfully touchy about some things. Like being touched. You could get away with saying a lot of things to them, but just don't muscle them around, you know? One of the gym teachers decided he didn't like that girl over there sitting on her boyfriend's lap. He grabbed her by the arm and pulled her off. She beat the hell out of him. Part of it was that he was white. Part of it was that he was a teacher. Part of it was that she was embarrassed in front of other kids. But what it boiled down to was that this big gym teacher got beat up by a girl. Everyone was left with one more hatred. A lousy situation all around.

Our only Negro vice principal worked that way. He was effective with some of the kids, in that he got them to behave the way he wanted them to. But behavior is such a shallow thing. Hell, I'd go through motions to avoid being slapped around. One of the problems with this whole system is that it rewards you for going through motions.

When the Black Power movement first began to rear its head in school, all the kids were wearing beads. Some of them were handsome—the ones made from nuts and seeds. Others were junky-looking. But they were an important badge, like the freedom cuts that had supplanted the greasy processes. One afternoon, a kid ran into Mr. Butler. He was livid with rage. When Mr. Butler asked him what the problem was, he said a teacher had said that only faggots wore necklaces. The boy was ready to kill.

"Well, I know what those beads mean," Butler said.

"Yeah?"

"Yeah. They mean you have pride. And I know I can count on a man with pride."

The fists unclenched. The kid's expression changed.

"Yeah, Mr. Butler. Put 'er there, Mr. Butler."

They shook on it. Real trouble may have been avoided. That was the least of it.

It's not all that hard to do the right thing. But it takes so much effort to think of the kid first, especially when you really need to explode. Arthur Wesson sat in my class for a month and never opened his mouth.

One day when I was feeling ugly, I asked him a question about the book we were reading. He didn't say a word. I thought of all the things I should have done, but no—I had to get belligerent. I asked the question again. Then I waited for an interminable length of time. Nothing.

"If you can't answer when you're spoken to, you can leave."

I hated the way I sounded. But I was too wrapped up in my own frustration to cope with anything Arthur might feel. He left. And I had to find out from a far more patient teacher than I that there wasn't anything personal in the kid's apathy. He couldn't read. His mother was insane, and there was no place to send her. The two babies at home hadn't eaten in a couple of days. I was just a very small ugliness in Arthur Wesson's ugly world. At least he'd found someone in school he could cry to. Except for selfishness, it might have been me. Every time I saw him, I hated myself all over again. I was too ashamed to look him in the eye.

If I can be redeemed, it is because, for all my mistakes, I did try to help. I did examine my failures. There was a Mr. Krantz who has never known shame.

He was the kind of man who let his mouth hang open as though his fleshy tongue were too big to be contained by it. Only when a thread of saliva slipped down his chin did he clamp his lips together. A slob. He taught gym, and he was sick and tired of these so-called intellectuals and their weird ideas about teaching. Because there's nothing to teaching but a few methods. And you can get them at any teacher's college. That's Mr. Krantz. He joined us with his doughnut and coffee one morning and said we had to hear this one—it was a real winner.

It all happened yesterday, after the baseball game. We'd lost, and on the bus coming home, Mr. Krantz just didn't like the way the boys were acting. They didn't seem to care about the loss as much as they should, you know? Now there's this one kid—Marrow—who's been askin' for it all year—you know the type—round glasses and beads and lotsa dumbass ideas. Anyway, he's in the back of the bus carrying on, and it just got to be more than Mr. Krantz could take. So he roughed him up a little, and even tore his uniform. And then he ripped off the kid's glasses and broke them in two and threw them out the window. He'd been aching to do that all year. And what's more, he finally told the kid he's sick of all his black power this and black power that. Mr. Krantz sat back in his chair and took a big bite of doughnut. The powdered sugar stuck to his mouth. He smiled.

Another gym teacher was sitting with us. Black.

"Do you react to this?" I asked him. I was shaking.

He said, "No comment."

To another teacher, black also, "Gloria, what's going on here? Why am I the only one who's upset?"

"Christ, baby, if I got upset over every little injustice in this place, I'd be crazy by now."

"You are telling the truth, aren't you?" I asked Krantz. "I mean, this really happened."

"Yeah," he said. "I don't know what you're so upset about. I feel like I'm on the defensive."

I assured him I didn't want to make him defensive, and I left. I couldn't stand watching the other man stare at his lap.

So things like this happen all the time. People get away with it, I learned, because "no one likes to make waves," and because in a school with no strong parent association and lots of tough kids, no one ever challenges the teacher. And where does it get you anyhow? I thought fleetingly of the Morris Feldman incident, and of the teachers who closed their doors to the trouble in the hall. I didn't know where it would get me, and I wanted terribly to find out what it meant to make waves. So I decided to make a big stink, just to see.

First I went to the kids to learn more about the incident on the bus, and to talk about teacher brutality in the school I'd thought was so special.

Eddie Albers explained, "Mr. Krantz, he crazy 'bout winnin' and if he don't win, he go berserk. I guess he kinda old to feel like that over a game, ya know?"

"Some teachers'll kill ya. They throw ya against the wall and hit ya, but you can tell they ain't serious. You can tell the difference when it happens to you."

"Most teachers ain't so bad, and the ones who are, you can kill 'em in June. But mostly, you just get to know their ways. You can take most anything, once you know their ways."

The kind of placid acceptance that makes life bearable for a lot of people annoys me. I can't stand the futility that causes it. Besides, a good fight is healthy—it gets your ulcers on the outside. It's awful, how so few people can enjoy one.

I went to Mike Marrow—the kid involved in the incident—and asked his permission to crusade in his behalf. He said it was all right, but his corner boys were already planning to take care of things. I tried to convince him that there were more effective ways of avenging yourself. He was tolerant, but unenthusiastic. Anyway, he agreed to hold his boys off till I'd seen the principal.

Butler was upset. It was a pleasure to find someone who shared my feelings. He talked at some length about racism and freaky people, and assured me he'd handle things. He spoke to Mr. Krantz that afternoon and called the boy in the next day to tell him about it. That was the beauty of his style. He was one of the only men I know who consistently met issues head on. Most adults would leave the kid out of the situation, explaining that it's better for him not to know certain things. But how much can silence protect a kid who's been beaten, humiliated, and exposed to the worst humanity has to offer? Krantz was apparently well trounced. Mike felt good—he'd been avenged. More important, though, was that he'd discovered the institution would stand up for him. Butler, in conferring with him, had treated him like a man. He felt like a big deal. He was so busy liking himself, there was hardly room to hate his coach.

Mr. Butler's tactics offend a lot of people. But they work—maybe that's what really bothers his critics. When the black activists were handing out a secret flier calling for a student walkout, Butler called an assembly. He had the flier in his hand.

"Some of you may not have seen this," he said. A bunch of teachers grabbed their heads and groaned. "I'll read it to you." He did. Then he went on to explain that the accusations, which had to do with the expulsion of certain students from school, were false.

"When there's something real to walk out of school for," he concluded, "we'll all walk out together. Until then, let's not make ourselves look silly."

At one that afternoon, students walked out of every high school in the city to attend a rally. North High alone was not represented. The kids were in class.

When the faculty-student demonstration did eventually happen, it was very satisfying. We had a cause. We had asked for an addition to the school—nothing big, just some classrooms and a gym. I'm never very excited about the money schools spend on athletic facilities, but it did seem wrong that our kids had to jump over holes in the floor and puddles from leaking pipes to throw a ball through a hoop. Especially when so many of the schools they visited were so shiny.

Our Mayor Tate explained that an addition to North was just not feasible. It would involve the displacement of fourteen families across the street. That's why. We reminded him that he'd left forty thousand black people homeless when he expanded Temple University, but he said this wasn't the same thing. This was a good Polish neighborhood.

It was hard to find anyone else to talk to. There was always city council, but our council was chaircd by a Mr. D'Ortona, who distinguished himself some time ago by addressing visiting delegates from Nigeria as "our visitors from Niggeria." Little slips like that didn't leave us with much assurance that this was a man we could count on.

It became impossible to deny that the North expansion issue was essentially racial. All around us, schools were building and buying land. It was North for which there were no feasible solutions. The one school in the city (and, I hope, the only one in the world) whose northern boundary was its front door—just fifty feet from that Polish neighborhood—and whose southern boundary was five miles away— at the point where the Black Belt ended and center city began.

It was an ideal crusade for Butler. It was his chance to prove himself to the kids; it was a maddening enough issue to enable him to mobilize the community; it was an opportunity to force a tsk-tsking public to recognize the injustice it allowed. And it was an ideal crusade because it could be won.

There was much fanfare. Five buses carted a parents' group to a school board meeting. The city council spent a day in school to Find Out a Few Things for Ourselves.

They marched around with television cameras and newsmen recording their every reaction. "Shocking," they said. "Appalling. We never knew it was this bad." They looked appropriately grave. They had to. This was their only chance to change their mind without losing face. And they had to change their mind. Butler was sitting on a bomb. The black community would not tolerate inaction.

It was an exciting day, and not without its personal satisfactions. When Morris Feldman heard that the TV cameras and councilmen had come to observe my class, he had a fit.

"Why did Butler have to take them to see that rabble-rouser!" he yelled at a group in the faculty lounge. "She's a lousy teacher anyway."

Shirly Master, whom I never credited with more than a nice wardrobe and a loud mouth, said, "How would you know if she's a lousy teacher, you pompous ass?"

What a marvelous day it was for us all. Shirly had made a friend. I got to gloat at Morris. The kids got more attention than a movie star. My mother, who saw me on television, got to tell me how awful I looked. North got its addition.

For all the excitement outside the classroom, my greatest concerns were still within it. It was the place where things happen in you, not just to you. And though I'd begun to look beyond the immediate problems of teaching five classes a day, I'd never stopped wrestling with the same old questions of what to do and how to carry it off.

I was never much of a scholar, but I'm a good critic and a good questioner. I'm even reasonably imaginative. These had become my tools in the classroom. My academic shortcomings, I think, are the very things that kept me from teaching a subject, and allowed me to teach people.

When I was asked how many years a senator served, I had already said "I don't know" to more questions than I could feel comfortable about. So I asked what the class thought. There were lots of ideas, and I wrote them on the board. Then, prefaced by a brief spiel on the glories of democracy, we had a vote. Four years won, and I announced that that was the length of a senator's term. It took them quite a while to decide why they were so uncomfortable about the whole thing. And Reginald Thompson finally said, "Can you really vote about something like that?" I looked at him like he was nuts. But Reginald went to the library for the first time in his life that day—and he looked it up!

As often as not, though, I stuck my foot down my throat. We were reading a story one day, and came across the name John L. Lewis. The kids asked me who he was. And since he seemed irrelevant to the issues of the story, I gave them a fast answer to shut them up. "Oh, he was the heavyweight boxing champ in 1922." It was a good ad lib, and we continued reading before the mood had been lost.

What I had overlooked, however, was a truth-telling footnote at the bottom of the page. All right—so I lied. The kids were hysterical. But I figured it kept them on their toes, which was justification enough.

Part of the art of teaching is the ability to rearrange the world for students—to force them to see things in a new way. I've known too many stupid intellectuals to believe that education and wisdom come as a package deal along with facts. It's your perspective that counts—your ability to see differently, not just to see a lot.

When I introduced them to Faulkner, I rewrote the story of the Civil War, painting it as the greatest atrocity in our country's history. I had them crying for the poor aristocrats, who were left floundering and slaveless, with nothing but their manners to hang on to. We agonized over the freed Negroes, who had no trades, no knowledge of city life or industrialization. They were better off on the plantations. We hated Abraham Lincoln for conniving to force the South into starting the war, merely to serve his own political ends. First, the kids fell for it; then they hated me for being an iconoclast; then they settled back into their hatred of Southerners and love of Lincoln. But they read Faulkner with a degree of understanding and compassion. They considered the source before jumping on a character who said nigger. After all, he was just a culturally deprived aristocrat.

When civil rights issues came up, it seemed smart to get out of the rut. So when a kid asked me why he was black, and another kid said he'd rather be white, I outdid myself:

When God decided to make man, he had all kinds of stuff he wanted to put into him—brains, fingers, smiles, hope, and a chemical called melanin—that's what colors your skin. When he made the first man, he used a heavy hand, like a new cook making his first stew. Since he was new at this business, he really didn't know what he was doing. So he threw in lots of everything—especially melanin. And the man was gorgeous—tall, strong, and shiny black.

Then God realized he'd have to go a little easier on his creations if he wanted to populate the whole world. So he used less of his substance in the second man—and he was brown. By the time he made Orientals, there was hardly any melanin left, although there was plenty of everything else. So the poor Easterners came out sort of yellow.

But when it came time to make the fourth man, the melanin supply was exhausted. So God figured he'd have to make do with what was left, and he created the white man. And ever since, white people have been smearing themselves with gook and frying in the sun to get black.

The kids are just as resourceful in their explanations of the world around them. When asked how the head of a political party gets millions of people to support him, Ruby Wilson said, "He beats them with the party whip." I had to agree.

In spite of the blunders, though, there is change. During our debate on black power, Raymond Dancey delivered a militant speech so convincing I was ready to convert. Ray was an extremist of the first degree, and he had explained to me long ago that there was going to be a revolution, and that he would be proud to die killing whites. He said he liked me a lot, but let's face it, I was just another white chick, and I, like the rest of my people, must pay for the centuries of enslavement I've inflicted on the black man. I suggested that as a leader of his people, he should try to build a better world— not a different kind of hell. He said there could be no better world till the black man had avenged himself. He's a scarey kid.

Anyway, his part in the debate was beautifully done. But his flash and style, though it moved me, didn't impress some of the other participants, who delivered very authoritative talks and asked very searching questions.

Ray listened for two days. When it was over, he approached my desk.

"You may not believe this, coming from me," he said, "but I don't know what I believe any more."

Neither do I. Teaching at North forces you to make choices and decisions that I just can't seem to make. Black people need group pride as well as a sense of individual worth. They need to identify with a culture that is theirs. But how?

Do we continue to run preschool classes where we teach two-year-olds to recite black catechisms like, "I want my freedom now by any means necessary"? Does the emotional climate created by such indoctrination lead to a sense of pride and identity, or does it spawn a nonreasoning, Nazi-type youth movement? I wonder whether it's possible to achieve anything without extremism—we rarely heed other tactics. Maybe they just don't work.

A friend of mine wondered aloud about the origin of umbrella stands, and like a shot, I told her that a Negro named W. C. Carter invented them on August 4, 1885. I felt like quite an authority, till everyone started to laugh.

"Where I teach, you have to know things like that," I offered. They kept laughing.

I guess they've got a point. Let's face it: we're overcompensating. In one grand act, Hitler gave the Jews six million martyrs to add to their five thousand years of tradition. Black people haven't been so lucky. The Negro history courses everybody's teaching and everybody's taking can, with very little effort, become glorified games of trivia. If we just had a sense of balance about it all, black people could find pride in the roles they've played in history and culture. But we haven't sense enough to integrate those roles in our teaching or our textbooks. Until recently, the black man never appeared in history books until the Civil War. Mr. Carver was the only Negro I ever learned about in high school.

But the pendulum has swung. The first man on United States soil was black. The first man to swim in the Pacific Ocean was black. If they told me Millard Fillmore's mother was black, I'd nod my head numbly. It's sickening how we make a joke of every decent thing we try to do.

While a few of the old biddies are still teaching manners comedies, you can walk into some other English and Social Studies classrooms and wonder if white people ever existed. Posters of Negroes are plastered on every wall, and the kids read Negro poetry, Negro plays, and Negro history. Only. The kids get seasick from the imbalance, but the teachers forge ahead undaunted. They beat their students blue with Pride and Identity.

More than anything, I'm confused. For a while, I had all the answers. It was a lot easier that way.

I remember people sing-songing, "Teaching is so rewarding!" Parents, uncles, advisers, and other spreaders of inspiration who'd never been in front of a class. "Teaching is so rewarding!" they'd glow, hoping, I guess, that I could be enticed to settle in what they thought was a nice, secure, ordinary job, and have Something to Fall Back On someday when I was a bored forty.

I doubt that I would include their pet word in a top-twenty list of words to characterize my job. Those daily occurrences that make you note, "Hey, that's a reward of teaching," just don't exist. When something gratifying happens, it's a subtle thing. And for every response you get, there are thirty other kids who just sit like vegetables. That tends to negate the pride of the moment. Once in a while, though, the skies part.

I had been having a good deal of trouble with a very slow class that just wouldn't open up. Because I'm me, I decided their quiet apathy was hostility, and I'd never be able to accomplish anything with a bunch of bastards who found me so offensive. There seemed little hope of getting them to speak, so we concentrated on those skills that didn't require any confrontations. We hardly looked at each other.

When we studied letter writing, I suggested that anyone who had trouble thinking up someone to address could write to me. It didn't matter what they said—just say it in sentences and think about spelling. You know, try to write.

I never got around to checking monumental things like punctuation. Every letter was written to me. And every one of them screamed with need until I couldn't stand it.

Dear Mrs Decker,
    I am this letter to let you know How I doing in your class. I know I am failing and I am trying to do my very best to get up But it seen hard. I have me a Job work in a move to go to all school. But it very hard you wound t underdand you not too Black. I have to take care my sister what little I make
    If I fail your class I would hade to go to summer school. and it would mess my hold summer work up. I am cloaing did litter to let you know That I will try my best.

It is a Very hurting feeling when You don't have a mother to cry to when thing are bad. And You two can sit down and make fun of Your father.

that's is What a mother is for to have fun with at time. I wish I had a mother so when I get marced she can say I brough my daughter up and she finded school.

That's is What I wish for Mrs Dieler that is Why I do some things wrong because I don't have a mother and I am not going to let no one run over me

Dear Decker

How you, fine I hope. I yell known and its all because or you. but know I got you where I wont you, and I wont you where I've got you because youre the one that kill my old grandpop. he sent me out to get you, he sent me out to killyou, and my friend, that what I going to do. so dont try to talk me out or it because my friend your luck is a thing or the past.

Joe was seventeen, going on thirty. I didn't know much about him, except that his dialect was particularly strange, and he couldn't read. He sat so close to the window his head nearly hung out—like he couldn't get far enough away from me. One day when I'd come into class late, Joe was writing on the board, "I WONT FREEDOM."

"Chances are you won't get anything till you learn how to spell it," I remarked. That was about the extent of our interaction.

His letter baffled me. People I showed it to advised me to give it to the cops or the principal. But for Christ's sake, get that kid out of the building.

Dear Mrs Mecker,
    I have a friend with a problem. I can't tell you her name. But here is the problem. She always come to me for advice, but not this. She's five months pregnant and wants to know if she should quit school now or wait until she is showing too much too stop. She also wants to know what might happen if the school found out. She says that she wants to finish school. I didn't tell her anything because I was afraid I would tell her the wrong thing. What should I tell her to do?

                                    signed
                                    Stuck

One after another. I learned that Billy Hancock's feelings were hurt because I didn't go to visit him when he was in jail—didn't I care? That Michele Morris got along okay with her stepfather till he raped her. That Hattie Simmons' father got mugged and the sons of bitches poked out both his eyes. That after Rita Torrent's mother died, her little brother never spoke again.

I went home that night and answered every letter. On stationery. I offered a couple of alternatives to Stuck, and told Joe that I was sorry for the awful thing I must have done to make him hate me so.

The next day I handed the pack of letters to Debra Fells for distribution. Her handwriting bore a striking similarity to Stuck's; I figured she could deliver her own letter more discreetly than I.

The kids' reactions were as overwhelming as their letters. They acted like they'd been clubbed over the head. Each sat, in his private shell, reading and rereading his note. The room was silent for an endless time. And when I finally began to teach, things were different. Gillis raised his hand for the first time all year. Rita smiled at me. It was a whole new thing.

A day or so later, there were two letters on my desk.

Mrs. Decker,

That girl I was telling you about is me. I had to tell someone. But now that I have I don't really know whether I have done the right thing. What do I do now?

Debra

Dear mrs Dectory
I am sorry that ~~~~~ I wrote
you a letter like that,
because I thing you is
much to nice person
to resoue a letter like
that. I sorry because ~~person and
thing~~ you is cuearful a ~~thing it is spell~~ rong
a verry good teacher and
a ~~very~~ verry fair one
unlike most teacher
so please forget about
that ~~letter~~ crazy letter
I wrote you befour ~~because~~
I didn mean it. please
look ouer the mice spell
words.
B your you mark ~~my paper~~
remember I try.

I took my cue and made a crafty conversion of a Kleenex box. The slit was just the right size. I brought it to school the next day and announced that any signed letters would be answered. Anything unsigned would be thoughtfully considered. For the rest of the year, friends, enemies, and desperate souls spoke through letters. It was probably the only unassigned writing they ever did. And since they wanted so much to be understood, their letters were great, laborious efforts at spelling and penmanship. The kids were their own best teachers, because they needed to know. I could just sit back and answer my mail.

Seeing change take place in young people is the greatest. By the same token, a kid with potential you just can't get to is frustrating enough to drive you up the walls. Michael Marrow was a slightly younger Byron Thurmond, just better-looking. Except for his run-in with Mr. Krantz, he was the darling of the school. He was handsome, charming, unusually well-spoken; it was just tough luck that he was a bum. Mike lived across the street from North. But he just couldn't manage to roll out of bed and into school until he got hungry at lunch time. That laziness routine gets very boring after a while. There are hundreds of kids who have an excuse a day: "Left my books on the bus." "Had to see my counselor." "Took my sister to the hospital." "Someone stole my ink pen." It doesn't take long to build up an immunity. But Michael Marrow had wormed his way under my skin. Like Byron, he was a kid I loved and hated. I spent hours with him talking about things, alternately trying to motivate and threaten. I offered to call his house at seven every morning, but he said his mom thought his first class was at ten, and she'd throw him out in the street if she knew.

I finally hauled him into Butler's office and explained that this was a kid who belonged in college and was getting F's in half his subjects. Butler was wonderful. He talked about black power and its leaders, and their college degrees. He ran through the same, enervating, half-hour of inspiration that he delivers to any kid who's proven himself a cop-out. Outside his office, a line of adults shook their heads and checked their watches. They'd just have to wait. Kids come first.

Michael was a new man when we left the office. He was excited and shaken and rung out. Butler had written a letter for Mike to give all his teachers, explaining that he was a college-bound student who would appreciate any extra work in order to make up what he had missed. The teachers would hate that note. It meant they'd be pressured into graduating one more undeserving kid.

With luck, the boy would produce for a while. The pressure would be justified. Butler always bet on long shots.

For no special reason, I was invited to attend a meeting at which Margaret Cox, a black-power leader, was speaking. I'm not crazy about meetings, but it occurred to me that it might be a good experience for the kids to hear a woman like her talk to a white group about black problems. The affair was to be held at a suburban synagogue, and when I suggested to the people in charge that I might be able to lure a few kids there, they were excited. There was to be a long question-and-answer period, and the kids would be able to air some of their ideas. They said it would be wonderful for the congregation. I said it would be great for the kids.

I approached my students tentatively. I felt bad about asking them to give up a Friday night, and I was concerned about putting them in an uncomfortable social situation. But the more I talked, the more eager I was to have them come. The kids who agreed to go fell into two camps—the ones involved in the movement, and the ones who liked me a lot. We arranged street corner pickup points and scheduled our four stops at five-minute intervals. I couldn't wait.

About an hour before Rob and I left home that Friday night, I panicked. They wouldn't show. I knew it. And I'd feel awful. I hated them—the whole impossible bunch.

At eight-thirty, we stopped at the corner of Broad and Vine to wait for Raymond Dancey. It was our only center city stop. Raymond was having some trouble with gangs, and said he couldn't wait on the street anywhere in his neighborhood. So he would take a subway into town. And he did! He was really there—with a tie in his pocket—he said he'd put it on if any of the others showed up in African clothes. He felt he ought to counteract them, since he didn't want the people to think all Negroes were alike.

I was still nervous, but it wasn't so bad now—I had Raymond. When we got to North Philly, great things began to happen—Sedrick was on his corner! And James Sytes and Moose and King on theirs—and Christabelle and Dorothy and Mike Marrow on theirs.

Wow. Sometimes they really pull through. Even Byron Thurmond. There were eleven of us in the car. The kids talked about dances and dates and cheap wine. It was fun.

We couldn't have staged our arrival at a better time. The adults were seated in eights at tables, drinking coffee, when we filed in. The kids looked great. The assemblage of African robes, shades, and leather jackets made a spectacular picture, and I loved being part of it—it appealed to my dramatic sense. I don't know what the congregation had anticipated, but I knew we had to be better then anything they could have imagined.

The speech was awful—full of vaguenesses and evasions and accusative remarks. I got bored fast, and spent a good deal of time stuffing myself with coffee and cake, hoping the kids would relax and do the same. They didn't. They sat ramrod straight and deathly silent, trying to keep their eyes on the speaker. I started to worry.

But when the discussion period began, the kids came alive. They listened for a while; when they got mad enough, they began to talk.

The meeting ended sometime around eleven-thirty, and I stood up to leave. Then, a remarkable thing happened. I pushed my way to the door and turned around to summon the kids—and they were gone! I retraced my steps and saw that each kid was surrounded by an attentive audience that was asking questions and listening while the kids mouthed off delightedly. It was a wonderful moment.

It was nearly one A.M. before the adults relinquished their lecturers. We piled into the car, and I got ready to ask all my questions. I never got the chance. The feedback was spontaneous. The awkward, dry evening I'd prepared them for had become a high point in their lives. They'd been treated like lords by a group of whites. They'd talked to people who wanted to listen to them. And they had learned.

"Man, I thought all rich people were smart," Mike said. "But they only know about books—they don't know nothin' about life."

"A white guy told me he'd never in his whole life talked to a black kid before."

"Yeah, me too—someone said that to me, too!"

"Hey, Byron—when you said 'revolution,' some of those white chicks fell off their chairs—man, they never recovered."

"I got a gig. Some Mr. Blumberg found out I can draw and gave me a gig in his advertising agency."

"Hey, teach—they acted like they really wanted to learn, ya know? Like they really cared about our ideas—"

All the way home!

One afternoon Earl Abner stuck his head through my door and said, "Can I be the godfather?" Three days later the doctor confirmed my condition. It wasn't the boy's incredible sixth sense that floored me—I've gotten used to that in the kids—it was the realization that I was under such close scrutiny.

"Well, you've been kinda cranky, and your face is rounder," my classes explained.

"But I haven't even told my mother yet!"

They chortled. They're very hip to pregnancy. Caroline Howard said that personally, she was relieved that I was pregnant, because there was a rumor that I couldn't have children. She just hoped I'd have an easier time than she had.

Fred Shiller was wide-eyed.

"I didn't think you could get pregnant," he said. "I heard your husband was a nonconformist."

Rubin Simpson asked what I wanted, and said he'd arrange it. The next day he announced I was going to have a boy.

"I worked roots for you, so you're set," he assured me. "But don't give me any trouble about grades and stuff, or I'll change it to a girl."

He had me in a corner. I promised.

I felt lousy knowing I'd be leaving in the spring. Butler makes you feel like a member of the family, and I was going to be a deserter. Besides, getting pregnant was such a horribly typical thing to do.

It also renders you somewhat of a lame duck—no one has to pay attention to your ideas when you're on your way out. I decided not to announce my leaving until I'd staged a crusade against Mr. Brown.

Mr. Brown is one of those useless, innocuous types who, had he been a nurse, would have said, "My goodness, we're looking perky today." He wears baggy brown pants and clumpy brown shoes. A tidy little mustache shines across his brown face. He is, however, super at shuffling papers. And since a super paper shuffler was what Mr. Butler needed to steer his Incentive Program, Mr. Brown had a job.

The Incentive Program was Butler's baby. It pushed the upper 10 per cent of the student body right into college, and bombarded them with courses they'd need to hold their own when they get there. For inspiration, there were Incentive teas for the parents, trips to homes of prominent Negroes, and tickets to every good show that came to town. Special counselors worked with these special kids on college applications, and scholarships aplenty were distributed by schools hungry to have a black or two. The program made it possible for Mr. Butler to announce to the press that North in two years had had a 300 per cent increase in the number of college-bound students. The fact that the school had doubled in size never seemed to occur to anyone, so Butler's statistics impressed us all—the kids, the public, and the government that picked up the tab for all those theater tickets. Few people asked how long these kids lasted in college either. A woman on the faculty who did a follow-up survey told me that 80 per cent of them were out by the end of the first semester. Which isn't all that discouraging when you consider the huge strides that have been made in just one generation. Many of the Incentive parents never finished high school. It isn't unreasonable to suppose that the children of our college dropouts will do their dropping out in graduate school. In the meantime, those kids have had a glimpse of college life and a taste of success—Butler saw to it that they felt very important. It was great for their ego, and that alone made the program worthwhile.

The problem with Mr. Brown was that he saw the Incentive Program as a means of ingratiating himself with Butler. There's nothing more nauseating or lethal than a yes man who gets ambitious. As the Dispenser of Federal Funds, he saw to it that Incentive students got everything from special books to special dances.

Our SCENES committee began to feel slighted. But since it's hard to get a straight answer out of a super paper shuffler, it took months to find out how slighted we really were.

What we eventually learned, when we actually wrested all those papers from Mr. Brown's hands, was that our budget had been cut from $8,000 to $1,200. H couldn't really tell us how it had happened, just that this was the way it was.

There wasn't any money for our corner boys and flunkers. There was, it seems, only money to pay a Cultural Director $6,000 to do the job we had done last year. Six thousand bucks to run a $1,200 program. There had to be some reasonable explanation. Of course—it was probably poverty money. Someone in Washington, I figured, had decided it would be nice to put one of the neighborhood ladies who knew the kids on salary, and feed her family while maintaining some skeletal program for the hard-core kids. I could buy that, sort of. But I resented working a program to the heights we'd achieved last year, and being thanked for my trouble and dismissed. All of us on the committee cared terribly about the kids we'd won over, and we didn't want to see what was left of the program flounder in a newcomer's hands. We decided that what we needed was not someone to do what five of us had done, but someone to relieve us of the ticket-ordering and poster-making chores that cut in on our teaching time. We'd refuse to disband, and maintain our link with the kids, getting them worked up enough to buy the few tickets there would be. Butler said O.K. It was wonderful that we were so interested.

Then we met Mrs. Cohen. No poverty case, she. She smiled a lipsticky smile under her rhinestone glasses and told us how hard it was for a middle-aged lady to amuse herself once the children were on their own. She just thought she'd go mad after the new apartment was finished, and wasn't it wonderful that she could have dear girls like us to work with a few days a week. She was sure we'd get to be great friends. Now down to business. Why, might she ask, had we ignored all those marvelous art shows and chamber-music concerts last year? She didn't want to suggest that we hadn't done a fine job, but didn't we realize what a wonderful experience real art would be for these poor children?

That was the beginning of the end. When the kids found out how our budget had been cut, they offered to pay more for tickets, if we'd just keep the program running. Hell, they'd pay a dollar each—that was only one lunch and a pack of smokes. But the Brown-Cohen alliance was more than we could fight. The good lady didn't care how little money we had, as long as it was "well spent"; and Mr. Brown just didn't care.

So, when five Incentive classes were treated to *Camelot*, courtesy of Mr. Brown's funds, I decided enough was enough. I requested a meeting with Mr. Butler, our committee, our Cultural Director, Mr. Brown, and all his papers. And I accused the worm of undermining us and pilfering our funds. Eyebrows shot up, papers rustled madly. Just because I'd said, "Mr. Brown, you're undermining us and pilfering our funds." I never really understood what the story was, but it appears that there is, somewhere, a Dispenser of Funds who programs the Mr. Browns of America. It's all his fault that the money got divided so unfairly.

It was a brief meeting, and Mr. Butler ended it by explaining in his gentlest way to the accused that for all my charm, I was not much of a diplomat. It was pretty embarrassing, but some valid inequities had been pointed up—it was true that Butler's program was overemphasizing the positive. Too bad it was too late. Facts is facts, and Mrs. Cohen was only one of them.

SCENES died a noisy but swift death. It was the first sad moment of the spring. Things got worse.

Rumors began to circulate about a union of black teachers that was planning to open the schools in September should there be a strike.

There'd been a lot of trouble about this forced-transfer business, and with reason.

No one wants to be shunted from school to school just to help balance racial scales. Teachers who, years ago, accepted a job under certain conditions should be able to expect those conditions to be maintained. Even if they really are bigots who basically just want to avoid teaching niggers. They'd be lousy in a ghetto school anyway.

But someone has to integrate the black faculties, if only to leave some openings for black teachers in white schools. Stalemate.

The stage was set for a reactionary group, and they came in on cue. The black teachers' organization decided that, since whites don't belong in a black school anyway, those in favor of forced transfers must be true enemies of black people, bent on destroying from within. Let's give black children the black images they need. Fight forced transfer with all you've got. Yippee.

You've got to be awfully careful these days—you might not stand where you think you stand. I mean, if I told my coworkers I was opposed to forced transfer, they might have thought I was a racist who wanted to preserve the status quo, or a radical who wanted to separate the races in order to build up a black nation within a nation. I mean, you're damned if you do, and damned if you don't.

Maybe I got pregnant at the right time. When people finally started to picket and everyone was picking sides, I'd be able to nurse my kid under a rock somewhere. That's a lot easier than resolving all the things you have to in order to make a commitment.

But September was far away, and April had troubles of its own.

Martin Luther King was dead. Mr. Butler got on the loudspeaker and announced that there would be a memorial service in the auditorium. Together we would mourn his passing. The choir would sing.

I resented the inaccuracy. The man didn't pass; he was murdered. And I certainly wasn't feeling placid enough to mourn anything. Besides, putting that choir on the stage is like programing you to cry. No one was going to play with me that way.

So I only stopped in for a moment. On stage, seated in high purple chairs, was the lineup: one principal, three vice principals, assorted department heads, and the other administrators. They all succeeded in looking as moribund as possible. The choir sang, and sure enough, everyone sniffed on cue. I thought it would be nice to be the sort of person who found comfort in such services. I would be spared the churning hatred that was making me sick.

Someone grasped my elbow.

"I want you to go up and tell Butler we want to speak."

It was Bob Handon. The whole crew stood behind him—Byron, Lawrence, Lamonte, and the rest. Several of them wore African clothes. Framed by their freedom cuts, their faces were stony. Only their eyes showed the violence and repugnance they felt. I looked at Bob again and thought a moment.

"I don't think I will do that."

It was all I could say. I couldn't explain that I, too, wanted to shake people into awareness of what had happened and what could happen. He didn't want my sympathy. Neither did he want any explanations about what a religious service meant to the majority of the two thousand participants, or what Mr. Butler was feeling himself, and his responsibility to keep the lid on a school that could have destroyed the city.

He glared at me, then stormed out of the auditorium. The clan followed, and I was at their heels.

The hall was hollow. Echoes of our footsteps and voices clattered against one another. It was chilly and dim, and a lousy place to be with those kids on that day. I leaned into a corner.

"Dig it, baby, that's a circus in there and it makes me sick."

"Could you believe all those honkies on the stage—our black brother gets shot by a honky and you honkies run a prayer service for him!"

"We should be running that meeting and getting those people together. But no—they got a bunch of honkies running a damn circus!"

They paced wildly back and forth across the marble floor. I said almost nothing. For nearly an hour, I was an object on which they could vent hostility. That was the most I could be for them. In coming to school that day, the militants were virtually begging for a legitimate forum in which to express themselves. It wasn't enough to break a window or cry. They needed to talk. I was disgusted with the administration for failing to anticipate this reaction to King's death.

The whole trouble with the institution is that it tells kids they should think, and then refuses to acknowledge or tolerate any new ideas. Basically, it's trying to teach you to function within it—not to change it. And it just isn't equipped to deal with any radical ideas. Which is why it's made such a mess of the militant kids. In coming to school at all, these kids are saying, "Hey, man, I need something! I'm mad. I'm confused. Do something with me!"

These are kids who have learned to express their hostility, to recognize their identity, and to seek change. They're as ripe as they come. And they're smart. But we haven't channeled any of their energies. The press, the principal, and the organizations have given them an exalted image of themselves. They're cocky.

Though small, the activist group has affected nearly every aspect of school life. It was they who organized the school's first black-power demonstration in the fall, and who made headlines in their march on the Board of Education. But their influence has been more strongly felt in quiet ways. They are making other kids think. The change in hair styles attests to that. They've made monkeys out of some of the faculty by challenging their methods of teaching and communicating with students. Teachers can't get away with pompous evasions any more. They can't give dumb assignments, because kids ask why. They can't hit and humiliate someone for "improper behavior," because kids won't take it. Our kids have learned to demand respect; they've learned to question the arbitrary rules of the old order; they've learned that they can force teachers to teach.

But power is never gained without concomitant abuses, and the faculty would use the blunders to Get Back at Those Snot Noses. You would hear them say, "It's going to give me great pleasure to fail that one," or, "I'm going to see to it that that kid pays for his rudeness." There was a good deal of bitterness. The old ones would fight change—it made too many demands on them. The young ones would destroy as much as they achieved—they weren't cool enough to keep from going off the deep end.

I didn't think I was entitled to respect or anything, just because I was a teacher. But as a human being, I resented the cruel treatment I got from some of this group. I'd take it from the kids who really believed I was guilty of the sins of the white world. But most of the kids could see beyond that business. They just got hung up on the fun of being mean; on the ego gratification that comes with putting down an adult; a teacher; a lady. And they got away with murder, because everyone was scared of them.

It was a difficult situation. It was hard to be on your toes all the time. I mean, it took effort to make every class creative and purposeful and all those other big words. So once in a while, I'd say, "You'll do the work because I assigned it." A kid would say, "Look, lady, I won't do anything that's not gonna teach me something." And I'd get mad, and he'd be right. A year ago, kids didn't talk like that. It's a great change. But it's hard to be on the receiving end. Lots of teachers just can't measure up. They've done nothing for so many years, it's impossible to start to move now.

So all that grows is hostility. I hated standing in an echo chamber of a hallway, listening to Byron—my old Byron—telling me how I felt and what I'd never understand. But I stood there like a jerk, because it seemed to me that that's what they needed—a jerky white to yell at. You've got to let people express hostility before you can channel it. But I was in no position to channel these kids. There were too many of them, and they would be allowed to storm out of the school when they were ready, and I wouldn't see them for days, or weeks. What a dumb setup. If we couldn't work with a small minority this year, we'd be in an even worse position next year when the masses began to polarize. Because our failures would be greater, we'd throw up defensive barriers; since we couldn't handle the behavioral changes in the kids, we'd certainly fail to treat their causes. And because their floundering would be as great as ours, they'd get louder and more active, to drown out the doubt. Together, we would ugly our way through the year.

By noon, most of the kids were tired of mourning. The whole situation had been talked to death. The gravity of the morning was lost in the normal lunch-time racket. I guess that's the way most of us get on with the business of living. My afternoon class didn't want to talk about it any more, but they were more than willing to react on paper. I asked them to spend the first few minutes of class writing anything they felt about the day and its mood. We'd been studying contemporary poetry, and I was amazed at the number of poems I got. It was as though poetry had provided them with a tool to express themselves, and a surprising number of them used it masterfully.

Martin Luther King was a man of peace. He died not to long ago. Now, we are fighting. For what? I don't know! Soon we'll all be at peace. We are dieing slowly.

The Time Is Near

One Night when I was siting on the porch step
I see a cat kill a mouse.

and I say to myself. Why don't he let him live?
Why don't Somebody stop him

Why do the cat pick on something so small
Don't he know that he will get the same chang as he gave
the mouse

and then I turn my head and walk away.
and say I will not make the same mistake

Because I will not put myself in a lower class. and
I will not show the world That they are better than me
I will show them that all men are
Created Equal.

death is slow coming
it nags
it makes you suffer
working, day in day out
paying bills
Rasing a family
Feeding them, clothing them
Some times you want to sit down,
and cry
why not. it helps.
well, atlease you think it dos
and they call death
Horribable
it's beautiful
for, see, with Death there arn't any
problems
live has no meanig for me!
and for the frist time I'm
happy!

In class, the kids were thoughtful and sad. Outside, things became depersonalized. A very popular white teacher was mugged in the corner drugstore. It was the kind of day that made you careful about touching kids you didn't know in the hall. For the first time in two years, I held the banister when I walked downstairs. I hated my discomfort, but the bitterness was too obvious to ignore. It was a day that left you with a backache.

The news of the spring was that Bob Handon had been offered a scholarship to Antioch. They wanted a black radical. The trouble was, he'd been to nearly none of his classes, and his teachers resented the pressure that was being exerted to pass him. Courses and grades are dumb enough—but when you pass a kid for doing nothing, you make yourself and the system look even sillier.

I'm embarrassed to sound so pompous. I hate hearing myself defend a system so in need of change. But for God's sake, you've got to demand *something* of a kid. Antioch would be great for Handon, and no system is worth depriving a kid of all that new world could offer him. But you just can't view him in isolation. What about all the dull, middle-class pluggers who come to school and work like hell. They've learned that succeeding in the system is the wrong way to make it; that their attention to scholarship and achievement has done nothing but earmark them for mediocrity. Hey, achievers, I don't care how poor you are, or what you've sacrificed to come to school and do the homework—you're dumb! You don't get to college by being a yesuh type, even if that's what we tell you to be. You succeed by spending Mondays picking out weird clothes, and Tuesdays upsetting a trial at city hall, and Wednesdays passing out fliers for a student walkout, and Thursdays smoking pot with some honkies and Fridays attending black-power meetings. That's life, baby. That's how you make it.

Handon's scholarship created a controversy as big as the school. I listened to people fight about it, but found no resolution, and no answers I could apply to my own smaller battles.

Byron Thurmond walked into my seventh-period class one warm afternoon.

"Lovely to see you," I said. "But it would be worth your while to visit me at nine A.M. when I can give you credit for your appearance."

"Oh, I'm not in your nine o'clock class anymore. I figured I couldn't pass in there."

"Well, that was pretty smart," I said. I wasn't even being sarcastic. Byron and I were beyond such games.

What I couldn't understand was his transferring into another of my classes—I mean, I'd already flunked him last year; he must have believed I'd do it again.

"You're a glutton for punishment." He smiled his we-have-rapport-and-we'll-fight-this-thing-together smile.

"I had to do a lot of talking to get into this class," he said.

"I'm flattered."

I was. I'd seen him only a few times since the Malcolm X record, and I felt bad that he hadn't been around to see how much I'd learned since last year. He might even have been inspired to get up for an early class.

I knew I was about to be put in a difficult position. This transfer was to be a clean slate, although he'd been absent for the past eight months. I would be expected to start all over again with him, just because he had a new class.

"What can I do to pass?"

He was right on cue. I was weary of that line. I wanted to tell him to forget the whole thing, but that wouldn't be fair to the other kids. So I told him to come to class regularly and catch up on all the reading since Christmas. He'd be delighted; I'd see he was a new man. We chatted for a while, and that was the end of Byron for two weeks.

It seems there had been a death in his family, and then his mother was sick. It was an unavoidable thing. And the books I'd assigned had been stolen, so he'd read some others and written reports for me.

The thing that made me mad was that the reports weren't even in his own handwriting. And I was insulted at his thinking I'd buy *Jane Eyre* and *Ivanhoe*. I screamed for a while and felt better, a little.

There was only a month left before grades closed for the year. I was very frantic about all I hadn't taught. I assigned *Manchild in the Promised Land*, banking on the kids' reading it, if only for the obscenities. I never cared what they read—it's the fact of reading and the issues you can build projects on that make for learning. I'd have given them comic books if nothing else would move them.

The last weeks of school are hard for everyone. It's just too pretty out, and school seems particularly dank and dreary. The school doesn't invest in books like *Manchild*, so I had to do a super job of selling it to the kids, not only to get them up for reading it, but also to inspire them to fork over a dollar to buy it. They've always got money for cigarettes, but talk about buying a book and they scream poverty. Unless they've never owned a book before and the novelty of it appeals to them.

I worked like hell. I read passages, and glamorized the ghetto, and played Bill Cosby records, and talked hippie. I even whined. They said O.K. So I ordered the book. Then came the hassle of collecting money. We elected a treasurer, which assured me of one sale—the treasurer has to set an example. Friends of the treasurer paid. I talked so much about it that a few kids brought money just to shut me up. They had that "All right, already, lady, here's your money—now lay off," attitude. There was always a group that did anything just because they liked me, and a couple who thought cooperation in such matters would help their grade. That left the stragglers. By then, everyone was so anxious to get the goods, they exerted pressure of their own—provided, of course, that you refused to give anyone a book till everyone had bought one. And for the two or three kids immune to even the point of Calvin Rush's knife, there was humiliation:

"It's all right," I said with incredible understanding, "I realize you have problems, and I know the class will help me buy you your book."

Down payments clinked onto my desk instantly. The dollars were paid in full by the next day.

I made much of presenting everyone with his book. It was an achievement for all of us.

I mimeographed a course of study which included all the issues and projects I'd extracted from the text. Not that they needed a copy, it's just that kids feel they're learning more when they can check off things as we do them. That way, a discussion becomes a topic covered instead of a daily chat. I was feeling like a real teacher. The kids read like mad, and the book became even more successful when other kids in school heard about it and started stealing it. To cut down on thefts, we covered the books with brown paper, which added a wonderfully risqué quality to the project.

We discussed and wrote about the author's life in Harlem, then moved on to a study of the ghetto, then studied our urban problems by researching in the library (a profitable experience—few of the kids knew what a card catalogue was). Finally, we constructed a model city. It was a pretty comprehensive unit. And I felt like a master; rarely had I been able to incorporate so much material in a related way. The only thing we didn't study in the book was vocabulary. The kids knew all those words, and there was no point in going over them simply for my edification. I talked a lot about how well the unit was going: they were reading fifty pages a week; they were doing successful group work to present oral reports; they were writing and talking and dealing with problems of the Negro family, the ghetto, crime, value systems, and the individual as a product of his society. It was great. They were great. I was great.

We finished the unit, I gave a test, and half the kids flunked.

Recriminations: Where had I gone wrong? If they hadn't learned, it was because I hadn't taught. Maybe they'd forged those reports. They hadn't read the book. I'd deluded myself. That's ridiculous. I knew they did the work. It was the test. It was a bad test. No, it's me. Help!

But there's never anyone who can help. You've got to find a way to live with the unanswered questions, and the failures. It's easy to get very negative about the whole thing. You never really know when you're being suckered. Whenever Chick Lind wanted to leave for a smoke, he had a sudden attack of nausea. His eyes got wide, and his cheeks puffed out, trying to contain the vomit. He waved his arms madly, and I ran to open the door for him so he could get to a bathroom in time. The other kids would break up. Now, was a kid like that going to read a four-hundred-page book? Not when he can get away with not reading it. The success of his weekly puking routine proved he could get away with anything. I always swore I wouldn't fall for it again—but he was so convincing!

So you begin to think everyone's wise to you. You don't dare refuse a girl a bathroom pass, even during a test. She'll tell you she's bleeding through her dress. And the one time I ignored a plea to be excused, the kid threw up all over the floor, then went into the hall and did it again in the water fountain, which got clogged up and overflowed. Water and vomit went spilling down the hall. The floor of my room stank with slime. And it was all my fault. I tried to ignore it and began to teach wildly. Within five minutes, three vice principals stood at my door. They watched the stream in the corridor, and the puddle on my floor, and my furious lesson. They seemed puzzled.

"Is there something we can do?" was all they ventured.

I felt awful.

"You can get a mop and clean it up."

Mike Marrow's empty seat had been insulting me all spring. His was a short-lived enthusiasm. I was hurt and fed up. He'd failed himself—it was his own damn fault. Senior grades had to be turned in soon, and Mike's only chance lay in a required make-up exam that every teacher had to give failing seniors. If they passed it, they graduated. I didn't like the whole idea. If a kid does nothing for a whole year, one test shouldn't squeeze him through. And my flunkers really had done nothing—no borderline cases, they. Theoretically, if the test covers the year's work, a truant can't possibly pass it. Pretty stupid setup.

I got a phone call very late one evening. A hushed voice announced itself as Mrs. Marrow, and she was speaking quietly so Mike wouldn't hear, you understand? She'd gotten a letter from some organization notifying her that her son had won a boy-of-the-year award, and it was going to be presented to him at this swanky hotel next month. She was so proud, but she didn't know why they'd pick Michael, except he's so charming and he's on the baseball team, but this really was a big moment in her life. She'd been alone for fifteen years now, and raised five boys, which is no easy job, especially when you work ten hours a day, but she'd done all she could for them. And since Michael talked about me all the time, she knew I had to be something special—why, she was even a little jealous of me, can you believe?—and would I do her the honor of going with her to the award ceremony? She didn't want to be alone there, and she would be so proud to have me with her.

I said I would love to.

She thanked me over and over, and apologized for calling so late, but she just didn't want Mike to know until the last minute. She was proud and all, but frankly, she didn't think that lousy kid deserved any awards, and it wouldn't do his fat head any good to think he was a big shot.

Mothers sure are funny people. I wanted Mrs. Marrow to see her son graduate—she deserved at least that. So I stooped lower than ever on the sucker scale. I offered to tutor the kid for his make-up exam. If he'd read two books in the next two weeks, I'd work with him on the other three items that would be on the test.

He had a reprieve. For a week, he told me how late he stayed up reading, and how he hadn't slept.

"Suffer," I said.

We both had the feeling he'd make it.

But two weeks was too long for Mike. He got through one book, and never showed up for his tutoring. He failed the exam. He failed the course.

I put off quitting until grades closed for the year. It seemed unfair for a substitute to give out final grades to kids who'd spent nine months working for me. Besides, I didn't want some alien messing with my kids. So I stayed until all those IBM sheets went back to their machine. I didn't look seven months' pregnant anyway.

Since last days should be special, I spent the night before baking cakes, one for every class. That way, no class would have to eat someone else's leftovers. Each group could have its own custom job.

Cake number one went along to my eight o'clock class. What a nice thing to do, I thought. But I'd been outclassed. I walked in on a catered affair. Eight A.M. and a baked ham. Macaroni salad. Forty cans of soda. Potato chips. Pretzels. Tuna fish. Potato salad. A tub of fried chicken (only wings—no necks, no backs). There were presents, too—new, soft baby things. And a huge bunch of roses. They were saggy and brown around the edges. A few cynics laughed at them, which put the kids who brought them up tight. That wasn't fair—especially since I didn't care that they were saggy and brown. They smelled great, and I'd feel pretty walking around with them. Two of the class matriarchs served the food—we all stood in line with the paper plates they handed us. It was a quiet line. We just stared at that incredible spread, thinking our own thoughts. I was wondering how I'd manage chicken wings and macaroni so soon after my first cup of coffee. I wondered all kinds of little things until I had to think about the big thing—that all of this had come from homes with so little. All this planning and shopping and cooking was for me. I was on the verge of getting corny. At eight A.M.

And that's the way it went all day. Food, presents, records and dancing, all beautifully organized and expertly carried off. The parties had been kept remarkably secret. The only one I'd suspected was my tenth-grade slows, who'd asked me to leave the room one day a couple of weeks before. I stood outside the closed door, and listened to the chatter turn into a din. Then Earl Abner's voice had torn through the racket as he assumed command.

"Listen!" he yelled. "We gotta get this thing together. I'm gonna make a list on the board and we'll just divide it up."

The room got quiet but Earl continued to yell. He was getting drunk with power.

"What we need number one is potato chips. How do you spell potato?"

I never saw so many potato chips as I did in that tenth-grade class. All the other trimmings were there, too. Althea Hendricks' aunt came to take my picture. At the end of the class, I was presented with the forty-five cents left from the food collection.

The good-bys were getting harder. You can't spend a double period every day with a bunch of kids without getting very involved with them. No, that's wrong. You can hate them. But if you don't, there's no in between. Slow kids get so dependent. It was good that I was so busy racing to the car for new cakes and unwrapping presents. Activity keeps you from getting maudlin.

It was a wonderful day, and not without its promises of good tomorrows. Byron Thurmond showed up in my last class to tell me he'd gotten out of a sick bed to come see me. Fat chance. He said he'd gotten turned on to college, and he was really going to make it this time. It was the most convincing, fervid speech he'd made in two years. Well worthy of a gesture on my part.

"I think we can agree that you're really semiliterate," I said.

He nodded.

"Spend three afternoons a week with me all summer, and we'll try to whip you into shape for college boards. I think it can be done. And if you stick it out, I'll come back in the fall and pass you for this year's work. What do you think?"

He was thrilled. No more playing around. College was for him. I was sure he meant it this time.

"What about math?" I asked.

"I had algebra for a week once."

"Well, how do you expect to apply to college without it?" I tried not to get screechy.

Byron patted my hand.

"Baby, you've got your summer cut out for you. You're gonna teach me English, and your old man's gonna teach me math."

I left fast when the bell rang. I was in a hurry to show Rob my presents and tell him about Byron. And I wanted to avoid the messy, long good-bys that would make me cry and embarrass everyone.

I just stopped for a moment to see Eli Butler. He was duly impressed by the stack of gifts piled under my chin. I wanted to hug him and tell him about two years. But we just shook hands warmly and said some nice things to each other.

It was a beautiful afternoon, and I could spend all those that would follow enjoying the sun. No more Sunday night pressures, or smelly corridors, or pay checks, or noise at the crack of dawn. I wasn't a teacher any more.

Some of the petals fell off my roses on the trip home, and I figured there wasn't much point in putting them in water—they'd never last the night.

I still don't feel like it's all over. I went to a perfectly vomitous faculty picnic late in June, sure that I'd seen everyone just the day before. And I got lots of phone calls.

Mike Marrow called to say he was going to summer school to make up my course, and he'd probably be able to start Temple University in September. He had two jobs, one for $2.40 an hour. In his eighteen years, I was the only person who'd gotten him to straighten out, and he was sorry I had to yell so much and flunk him in order to do it. Could he take us out to dinner on Friday night.

There were other calls too. None of them surprised me as much as Frankie Horn's.

"I'm living in Newark," he said. "And I'm working and finishing school. I think I'm gonna be an architecture, like your husband. Maybe if I come to see you sometime, he can lend me some books."

I said that sounded great, but he was rotten to drop out of my life for so many months.

"Well, things were tough for a while with my Mom and the kids and all," he said. "But you know I wouldn't forget you after all you did for me. How could I ever forget you?"

I agreed that I was hard to forget.

I never heard from Byron. One of the kids who called told me he'd had a job for a few days, but they made him do janitorial work, and he couldn't hack it. I couldn't believe that anyone would tell a guy like that to clean floors. I was glad he'd quit. But was he doing anything else? The boy on the line said no. Goddamn him. What a waste. The army will get him for sure, now. He would have had a good deal with me as a tutor. But three days a week is a grueling routine for a guy who's lived on charm for twenty years. He probably couldn't have stuck with it anyway.

It's just as well. My time is my own now. I can go to the shore any day I please.

About the Author

Sunny Decker was born in Philadelphia and grew up in nearby Lower Merion. She was an honors major in English at the University of Pennsylvania and married a graduate student in architecture, Robert Decker, the day before graduation.

Mrs. Decker attended graduate school at Temple University and taught in the North Philadelphia ghetto area for two years. The Deckers' son, David Jeremy, was born on September 5, 1968.